Overlems

Coping with Compulsive Eating

RUTH SEARLE

sheldon PRESS

First published in Great Britain in 2007

Sheldon Press
36 Causton Street
London SW1P 4ST

Copyright © Ruth Searle 2007

The author and publisher have made every effort to ensure that the
external website and email addresses included in this book are correct and
up to date at the time of going to press. The author and publisher are not
responsible for the content, quality or continuing accessibility of the sites.

British Library Cataloguing-in-Publication Data
A catalogue record for this book is available from the British Library

ISBN 978–1–84709–010–2

1 3 5 7 9 10 8 6 4 2

Typeset by Fakenham Photosetting Ltd, Fakenham, Norfolk
Printed in Great Britain by Ashford Colour Press

Contents

About the author

Ruth Searle began her career as a nurse and midwife and, although her love of nursing has remained constant, she went on to fulfil her dream of becoming a marine biologist. She completed her PhD on humpback whale behaviour and is continuing with field research that takes her around the world. Passionate about nature, wildlife and conservation, she writes about the subjects she loves, including marine biology and the humpback whale. Ruth confesses to being 'hooked' on studying and has almost completed a second degree in Earth sciences, cosmology and particle physics, and she plans to study philosophy next. Her triumphs and struggles to find and live her own personal dreams provided the inspiration for *The Thinking Person's Guide to Happiness*, also published by Sheldon Press.

Introduction

First, I want to tell you that if you have problems around food, you are not neurotic, psychotic or in any way abnormal. You are a victim of modern life, and there is a way out whereby you can regain total control of your eating and make decisions about your diet, free from the cravings that characterize compulsive overeating and bulimia. You can lose weight without ever dieting again, regain control in social situations and never again let food control your life. I hope and believe that this book will help you feel well without the lethargy, headaches, stomach problems, fuzzy thinking, depression and loneliness you are likely to have been experiencing, maybe for years. If you will stay with me throughout the book and try the solutions I have to offer, you can end the struggle and break free of compulsive overeating and bulimia for ever.

I believe that the current thinking around compulsive eating and bulimia is completely missing the point, and while psychological issues may well contribute to the problems of compulsive overeating, this is by no means the principal causative factor. Indeed, the preoccupation with psychological causes may well even exacerbate the problem and contribute to the isolation, embarrassment and shame that many feel. There are more compelling and fundamental reasons why people overeat, and these are physical and physiological triggers linked to the way our bodies are trying to cope with a modern diet.

In this book we will explore together the reasons why we have developed problems with food, the physiological causes of overeating, how we can regain control within days with a vital first line of treatment and then, with a clear mind, make the right decisions about our diet in the future. We will discover how easy it can be to lose weight and maintain it for a lifetime without dieting.

All I ask is that you read the whole book, not just the chapter that sets out what you should eat and how to lose weight without dieting. There is a very good reason for this. I want to show you how you can 'love yourself better' and feel healthy and totally in control by understanding the problem thoroughly, forgiving the past and changing the way you think about food and your psychological associations with it. I want to help you challenge your beliefs, find strategies for coping with the social pressures to overeat and learn to love your body and look after it as the life-support system it really is for you – not just for now but for the rest of your life.

Acknowledgements

I would like to thank Robert Patterson for his patient counselling and for setting me on the road to recovery. Fiona Marshall and the editorial and production teams at Sheldon Press also have my thanks for their help in producing this book.

Part 1

UNDERSTANDING THE PROBLEM

1

What is compulsive eating?

Compulsive overeating, or binge eating disorder, is distinct from simple overeating and is defined as an addiction, obsession or preoccupation with food. Someone who is a compulsive overeater engages in regular uncontrolled episodes where large amounts of calories are consumed, often quickly and at one sitting (binge eating), but sometimes by continual overeating throughout the day (compulsive eating). Overeating usually happens in secret and is associated with intense feelings of guilt, shame, remorse, loneliness and depression.

The signs of compulsive overeating are:

- eating uncontrollably;
- eating unusually large amounts of food at one time;
- eating more rapidly than normal;
- eating until uncomfortably full;
- eating alone and secretly;
- preoccupation with food and body weight;
- awareness that eating patterns are abnormal;
- history of dieting;
- feelings of shame, guilt, remorse and embarrassment;
- depression;
- social withdrawal.

Many compulsive overeaters have low self-esteem and have a constant need for love and validation that they try to satisfy with food. Childhood conditioning and eating patterns may mark the onset of compulsive eating, and many compulsive eaters have not learned to cope effectively with stress, turning instead to food as a comfort and a mechanism for blocking painful emotions.

Compulsive eating and binge eating inevitably lead to obesity, although some people who overeat may impose ever stricter rules and regulations about eating in an attempt to regain control. Some compensate by dieting, starving themselves, exercising excessively or using laxatives, although many do not do this.

Bulimia, which is considered a variation of compulsive eating, may develop, where overeating is compensated for by purging and making oneself sick in an effort to regain some control. Bulimics are often of normal weight or slightly overweight. It has been estimated that bulimia affects between four and ten per cent of women and five per cent of men, although reliable figures are notoriously difficult to obtain. The condition may be much more widespread than is currently known. Bulimia itself causes food craving and overeating, and a vicious circle of bingeing, purging and dieting can ensue that is extremely hard to break.

Compulsive overeating, if left untreated, can lead to serious medical conditions, including:

- diabetes
- high cholesterol
- hypertension
- heart disease
- certain cancers
- clinical depression.

Long-term effects also include kidney disease, osteoarthritis and stroke.

Compulsive eating disorder is difficult to categorize or define as it does not fit neatly into a disorder category. It is not a true obsessive–compulsive disorder, an addictive disorder or an affective disorder. Compulsive eaters are generally normal people psychologically, and bulimics are often highly intelligent, successful people. They are not lacking in will-power nor are they gluttons.

Treatment

The good news is that compulsive eating disorders can be treated successfully and overcome when treatment is sought. And there are powerful ways that you can tackle the problem yourself.

Treatment-wise, it's not a clear picture. There is no definitive known cause for compulsive eating disorders or bulimia, and research is ongoing into both the causes and the treatment. Thus there seems to be no consensus of medical or scientific opinion as to the most successful treatments, and various methods can have equally beneficial effects.

Professionals' treatment of choice for compulsive eating and bulimia is generally cognitive behavioural therapy, which attempts to replace dysfunctional habits with healthy ones. It can be effective, and some long-term successes have been achieved. However, this preoccupation with compulsive eating and bulimia as psychological disorders overlooks the powerful physiological and physical triggers that are even more compelling.

Why our diet may be unsuitable

It may well be that, rather than compulsive eating being 'all in the mind', there is an actual history of eating that has led us directly to our present position. Our bodies can become sensitive to the overprocessed diet of modern man, which in evolutionary terms has come about very rapidly. Some 10,000 years ago – a mere blink of an eye in terms of overall evolutionary development – humans invented agriculture and began to modify the food they had been eating, which eventually led to the highly processed and sugar-rich diet we consume today. Prior to the Agricultural Revolution, during the Palaeolithic era, humans ate a diet of wild plants and animals. The Palaeolithic era endured for about two million years, and during that time the human body became genetically adapted through evolution to process a natural hunter-gatherer type diet.

Since the Agricultural Revolution, human genetics have scarcely changed, and modern man has had far too little time in which to adapt genetically to such enormous changes in diet. Many experts believe it is this that is causing the so-called diseases of civilization as well as physiological and metabolic maladaptions. Conditions implicated in this include coeliac disease and other gastrointestinal disorders, forms of dermatitis, gluten cerebella ataxia and other diseases as diverse as multiple sclerosis, schizophrenia, chronic fatigue and attention deficit disorder. Diabetes, insulin sensitivity and a collection of conditions known as Syndrome X are also thought to be caused by our modern diet (we will explore some of these more fully later).

Physiological imbalances can lead to food addictions and food intolerance as well as the more serious food allergies. The chemical imbalances and food addictions that result from an unsuitable diet can take a hold on the body as powerfully as heroin, alcohol and nicotine addictions. Will-power is not enough to control addictions, as any smoker or heroin user will verify. But if you take this 'history of eating' into account, it is no wonder that compulsive overeating is so widespread in the modern world, and so difficult to combat.

However, with the right approach compulsive overeaters and bulimics can become free of food addictions and regain control. Without the appalling cravings for food, overeaters can begin to control and plan their eating once again and make healthy choices. They can also work on their relationship with food and understand any psychological triggers that have contributed to their overeating. But until these powerful addictions are tackled it may be impossible to regain control, making the vicious circle of overeating and overcompensating for it more deeply engrained than ever, while reinforcing negative behavioural patterns associated with assumed psychological triggers.

Food addictions

Food addictions are difficult to deal with because while other substances such as heroin, alcohol and nicotine can be eradicated from the body so that the cravings can be controlled, we cannot live without food. Everyone will have different food addictions and triggers that lead to compulsive overeating, and this of course complicates any standard treatment; but there are some main culprits in our diet that can be assumed to be triggers for all modern humans, and these are generally processed modern foods that we can happily survive without. There will be much more on this later.

Dieting

Compulsive eaters generally have a history of dieting, yet diets do not work for the majority of people, and lead inevitably to a regaining of the weight lost plus some extra. Dieting can even be the trigger for eating disorders, depression, anxiety and social withdrawal. Again, there are physiological reasons for this that are also rooted in our genetic history. Dieting depresses the resting metabolic rate because the body receives signals that it is being starved and so protects its fat stores. This is a response that was life-saving in our ancient ancestors when food supplies were often unpredictable. This is why on any diet, you put weight back on as soon as the diet stops, which can lead to yo-yo dieting that is so very damaging to health.

Regaining control

I hope and believe that the approach in this book will allow you to stop dieting for ever and lose weight. By following a lifetime plan free of food addictions or dieting, you can lose weight naturally and keep it off permanently without the heartache and misery of fighting against compulsive eating and bulimia.

You can overcome food addictions, compulsive eating and cycles of bingeing and starving – often within days – and regain complete control over your food intake, maybe for the first time in years. The first line of treatment set out in this book is designed to eradicate cravings and get you back in control so that you can tackle the social and psychological triggers for overeating free of addictive cravings and with a clear mind.

Once you have control, you can begin to put in place a long-term plan of eating and exercise that suits you personally. Exercise is always advocated in any weight-loss plan as a means of 'spending' calories, but in reality you'd have to run about ten miles just to burn off one average bar of chocolate! Exercise is far more useful as a means of stress control, balancing the body's physiology, relaxation, motivation and appetite control. It also helps the body cells to burn glucose and plays a role in maintaining weight loss permanently. Moderate exercise is also invaluable as a means of taking some time for yourself, and we will be looking at ways to exercise that help you to feel good. Don't worry – it needn't be a chore.

While in reality psychological issues may not have the importance they have traditionally been given in both the causes and the treatment of compulsive eating and bulimia, they may well contribute to the problems and to the habits of overeating. It is important to address these triggers as well as find strategies to overcome the considerable social pressures that contribute to overeating. Many overeaters have low self-esteem, and until this is remedied it is difficult to overcome psychological difficulties. We will look at ways to increase self-esteem and assertiveness when we explore your lifetime plan in Part 2 of this book. You really can love yourself better with a change in your thinking.

2

What we eat

Before we look at food and the way our bodies utilize it – and subsequently object to the wrong sort of food with food cravings – I want you to make a list of your favourite food. That is, the sort of food you eat most days; just a typical intake for a typical week. Fill in the chart in Exercise 1 (overleaf), or devise a list of your own. This will be used later when we come to plan your perfect diet, but for now just make a note of all the foods you like. No one will judge this list so be completely honest so that you can work on a suitable action plan later.

Once you've done that, put the list away. You will need it again, but for now we'll have a look at the way our body uses the fuel we put into it and what can happen when the natural pattern is upset by overeating the wrong foods.

Your life support system

The fuel our bodies need is in the form of carbohydrate, fat and protein (with vitamins and minerals in small amounts). Everything we eat is one or a combination of these. In order to create a plan to overcome the problem of compulsive overeating and bulimia, we need to understand the basics of the way our body uses food and how it reacts when we give it the wrong foods.

Our bodies need food as a fuel for energy and to keep us warm. It provides the minerals and vitamins we need for the growth and repair of tissues and for the chemical processes that take place to keep us alive. The energy obtained from the food we eat is in the form of calories. Two-thirds of the energy we need is used to maintain normal body temperature, to maintain muscle tone, keep our hearts beating and keep other organs functioning normally. This is our basal metabolic rate and if we did nothing but sit in a chair all day we would need this energy

Exercise: What food do you eat?

	Typical foods/drinks
Breakfast	
Mid-morning snack	
Lunch	
Afternoon snacks	
Evening meal	
Evening snacks	
Drinks throughout the day	
Favourite foods	
Foods you tend to binge on or overeat	
Foods you could never live without	

	Times
When you tend to overeat (all day, evenings, etc.)	

to keep going. It equates to approximately 1,600 calories a day for an average 10 stone (64 kg) adult. The rest of the energy we need is for moving about, exercise and working, and it comes from the other third of the calories we take in, or around 800 calories in this example. The more energy we use, the more extra calories we need, and when we take in more calories than we need, they are stored as body fat.

Carbohydrates

Carbohydrates come in many different categories but can essentially be described as unprocessed or processed (refined) carbohydrates. The unprocessed carbohydrates are the natural foods, such as vegetables and fruit, that can be picked from trees and bushes or dug up from the ground and eaten in their natural state or cooked without adding anything but water (baking, boiling, steaming, grilling). For example, potato chips are not natural because they have been processed and cooked in fat; orange juice is not natural because it has been processed and is no longer in its natural state as a whole orange. Natural unprocessed carbohydrates include jacket potatoes, whole fruit and vegetables. Processed carbohydrates include the enormous variety of convenience foods available including cakes, puddings, pastries, jams, biscuits, sweets, pizzas, chips, pastas, cereals, etc.

Carbohydrates are foods that are most easily converted into glucose fuel for the body to use as energy, and they are found in sugars, starches and cellulose.

Fats

Fat comes from animals in the form of meat, fish, cheese, eggs, cream, milk and other dairy foods. They are solid at room temperature. Fats are also obtained from vegetables sources, for example groundnut (peanut) oil, olive oil, sunflower oil and vegetable oil, which are generally liquid at room temperature.

Fats can be categorized as saturated fat, monounsaturated fat, polyunsaturated fat and transunsaturated fat. Fats improve the palatability of food, making it easier to chew and swallow as well as improving the taste. Fats are concentrated sources of energy, providing more than twice the energy for weight of either carbohydrates or proteins. Vitamins A, D, E and K are found in fat and are fat-soluble – in other words, these vitamins require fat in order to be absorbed into the body.

Saturated fats are the fats that the body uses for energy and are found mainly in dairy products such as cheese, butter, cream, whole milk and fatty meat (the meat of grain-fed farm animals is full of saturated fat compared to the meat of wild animals, which is lean). They are known to raise cholesterol and can be deposited as fatty tissue or plaques on the artery walls, leading to heart disease.

Monounsaturated fats are good fats found in olive oil, nuts and avocados. They lower blood cholesterol and help prevent arteries clogging up with fatty plaques.

Polyunsaturated fats are mixed. Some are good, such as omega-3 polyunsaturated fatty acids, found in oily fish such as mackerel and salmon, while others are not so good, such as the omega-6 polyunsaturated fats found in vegetable oils, shortening in baked foods and in many processed foods. Omega-6 fats are bad to eat at the expense of omega-3 fats. We need a balance of these for health. The good fats, omega-3 fatty acids, are essential fats used for building cell membranes, for healthy nerve and brain function and for bone formation. We rarely eat enough omega-3 fatty acids.

Transunsaturated fats also called trans-fatty acids or TFAs, are found in hydrogenated oils, margarine and shortening in biscuits, cakes and nearly all processed foods – in other words, the processed fats and oils rather than the natural fats such as butter or olive oil. TFAs are the 'bad' fats and can be extremely harmful. These, along with a high intake of saturated fats, are very unhealthy for the human body, considerably increasing the risk of heart disease, diabetes, certain cancers and obesity.

Protein
Protein comes from animal sources such as meat, fish, eggs, cheese and other dairy foods and also from vegetables such as nuts, wholegrains, beans, pulses and tofu.

Proteins are essential for building and repairing all body tissues: brain and nervous tissue, bones, muscles and organs. When there is not enough protein in the diet to make up for the normal breakdown and loss of tissue, the body breaks down some of its own less vital protein, such as muscle, in order to protect vital organs such as the brain, heart and kidneys. We generally obtain enough protein in our diet for normal requirements but in times of illness or stress we need more protein than usual.

Meat is a combination of fat and protein. Lean meat, such as that found in wild game and seafood, is about 80 per cent protein and 20 per cent fat, but farmed meat such as lamb is very fatty and contains about 75 per cent fat to 25 per cent protein. Despite the warnings that red meat is bad for us, it is actually the saturated fat in some meat that is bad for us, not the meat protein. Lean protein is essential for health.

The combination of carbohydrate, fat and protein

Meat and fish have no carbohydrate and are composed of protein and fat in varying proportions, depending on the cut and how lean they are. Butter and oils are almost all fat, with a trace of protein. Fruit and vegetables are mostly carbohydrate, with a trace of protein and fat, and both milk and nuts are a good combination of all three. Most other foods are a combination of carbohydrate, fat and protein.

It is important to remember that *all* the foods we eat are a combination of carbohydrate, fat and protein. When you opt for a low-fat food at the supermarket you are effectively buying a high-carbohydrate one because if the fat in a food is reduced, then there has to be some other substance (either carbohydrate or protein) to replace it, otherwise you'd be left with nothing! Manufacturers generally replace fat with sugar. Check the sugar content in, say, a low-fat yoghurt against a full-fat one. The sugar content is higher in the low-fat yoghurt. As long as you are aware of this, you can make an informed choice about the foods you buy.

How our bodies process the food we eat

The gastrointestinal system is basically a hollow tube approximately 4.5 m (15 ft) long running through the body from the mouth to the anus. The tube is continuous with the external environment and so the contents of the tract are technically outside the body. This allows the millions of bacteria, including those damaging to our health, to live in our large intestine, which, although harmless there, would be detrimental and even lethal if they entered the internal environment of your body, for example from a ruptured appendix. Food taken in from the mouth must be broken down into individual molecules such as amino acids and monosaccharides by the process of digestion. This is accomplished by the secretion of hydrochloric acid, bile and various digestive enzymes from the digestive glands of the gastrointestinal system. The molecules left after digestion are moved through the gut by the contraction of muscles in the gut wall. They pass across a layer of epithelial cells into the blood or lymphatic systems by absorption. Therefore the function of the gastrointestinal tract is the storage, digestion, absorption and motility of food. The motivation to eat and hunger signals are part of the internal environment of the body.

3

Motivations for eating and drinking

In order to understand what can go wrong with our normal need for food, it might be helpful to understand how our body motivates us to drink and eat.

Psychologists use the term motivation to describe the driving force behind an action or behaviour as well as its strength and the persistence of the behaviour. Our biological needs prompt us to respond to motivations as a survival mechanism. We need air, water, food and protection from extremes of temperature in order to survive, and all complex organisms have mechanisms that regulate their physiological processes. Behaviour is one such mechanism, and eating, drinking, finding food, shelter or warmth are behavioural regulators that adjust our physiological balance. Hunger and thirst are the driving forces that motivate us to seek food or water, and are the body's way of correcting physiological imbalance. When we seek food or water to satisfy these drives, they are subdued when our hunger or thirst diminishes. We experience these motivations on a regular basis and we know them well, but what actually causes thirst or hunger?

Thirst

Up to 70 per cent of our body is pure water: over 85 per cent of our blood, 70 per cent of our muscle and 75 per cent of our brain consist of water. Water makes up most of our cell volume and it surrounds every cell in our body. It lubricates, cools, acts as a solvent and a means of transport in our bodies and maintains blood and lymph volume. It regulates our temperature, carries nutrients, removes wastes and facilitates the billions of chemical and metabolic reactions that take place every millisecond.

As we use up our fluid reserves by perspiring, passing urine or during breathing, we lose water from two reserves within the body: within the cells (intracellular fluid) and outside the cells (extracellular fluid). When water becomes really low in our bodies, our muscles lose the ability to contract; brain function fails, with a loss of concentration and slow reactions; toxic chemicals accumulate and cell function is impaired so that fatigue and confusion result. When we drink, we should drink pure water. Sugary soft drinks add unnecessary calories and escalate the problem of obesity, while caffeinated drinks are slightly dehydrating, which only further increases our need for water.

Osmometric thirst

Osmometric thirst is caused by dehydration within the cells of the body. Cells contain intracellular fluid, which includes water, protein, fat, carbohydrates, sodium, potassium and other substances. Intracellular fluid makes up about 40 per cent of the total body weight. Outside the cells, the body contains fluids both surrounding the cells and as blood plasma in the circulatory system. This extracellular fluid makes up about 20 per cent of the body weight. When the salt solution in the extracellular fluid surrounding the cells is higher than the salt concentration within the cells, the water is drawn out of the cells by a process known as osmosis, and dehydration subsequently occurs within the cells. We feel thirsty because special neural cells associated with the central nervous system, called osmoreceptors, which are located in the brain, detect this dehydration. Our nervous system responds and motivates us to drink water in order to dilute the salty extracellular fluid and allow water to diffuse back into the cells to restore the correct fluid balance. This is why you feel thirsty after eating salty foods and why patients on intravenous infusions are given fluids with electrolytes, so that the correct salt concentration is maintained within the cells.

Volumetric thirst

When there is a reduction in the extracellular fluid, such as when blood plasma is lost due to bleeding, we experience volumetric thirst. This can also happen when there is too little salt in the diet, because when intracellular fluid becomes more concentrated than extracellular fluid, water is drawn into the cells by osmosis, effectively depleting the extracellular fluid. It is the kidney that regulates volumetric thirst by detecting the volume of blood flowing to the kidney. If blood flow is reduced, the kidneys release enzymes that produce hormone messengers that motivate us to drink. There are also receptors – called baroreceptors – in the blood vessels that detect a reduction in blood pressure. When this happens, the baroreceptors motivate us to drink via the central nervous system.

Hunger

The incentive to eat is caused by an interaction between the physiological need to eat and gain energy for our body and brain, and the taste of food and the pleasure it gives us.

Physiological hunger

Surprisingly, the feeling of hunger does not actually originate in the stomach. People who have had their stomachs surgically removed because of tumours or large ulcers and have had the oesophagus attached directly to the small intestine (requiring small frequent meals) still feel hunger and the satiation of hunger just as they did before the operation. It seems that the feeling of hunger and the motivation to eat comes from the depletion of the body's nutrient stores, not from an empty stomach.

Our cells use glucose and fatty acids as a primary fuel obtained from carbohydrates and fat in the diet (see Figure 1, overleaf). Carbohydrates form a short-term store of nutrients; fats a long-term store.

When glucose is obtained from our food, some of it is used as fuel and some is stored in the form of glycogen in the liver as a short-term reservoir of nutrients. Fat is stored as triglycerides in the fat cells beneath the skin and around the abdomen, and functions as a long-term store of nutrients. When the glycogen stores from the liver become low, fat cells start to break down and release fatty acids and glycerol (a form of carbohydrate).

Our brain runs on glucose, and when glucose is depleted in our bloodstream the liver converts glycogen back to glucose for use by the brain. When this runs low, the fat cells release glycerol, which is

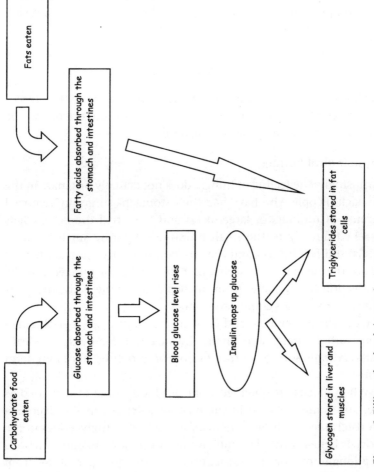

Figure 1 Filling the body's nutrient stores

also converted into glucose so that the brain, a most vital organ, is always nourished even when the short-term reservoir of nutrients becomes low.

The rest of the body needs fatty acids, which are obtained from triglycerides in the fat tissue, and also glucose for energy. Figure 2 is a schematic diagram representing this system of food metabolism.

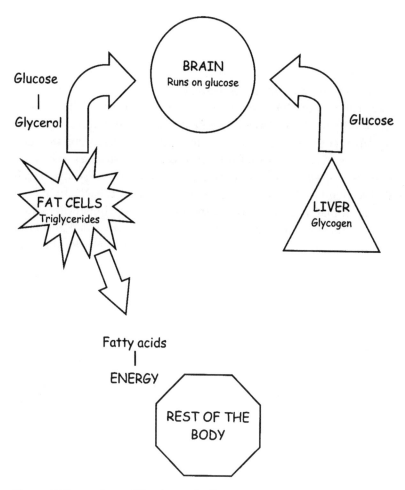

Figure 2 The system of food metabolism

As you can see, glucose is vital for brain function, and it is thought that hunger occurs when the level of glucose in the blood falls below a certain level, probably when the short-term store of glycogen has been used. This hypothesis is known as the glucostatic hypothesis of hunger. The decrease in blood sugar is detected by glucostats, which are glucose-sensitive neurons in the brain. It appears, then, that hunger originates in the brain rather than the stomach as might be expected from the feeling of hunger we experience. But what is responsible for telling us when to stop eating?

Feeling full

It takes about an hour or more for nutrients to be broken down and begin entering the bloodstream following a meal. However, your body needs a more immediate way of detecting when you have eaten enough or your stomach would not be able to hold all the food you would have to eat before satiation detectors in your bloodstream told you to stop eating. This is where your stomach is important. It seems that the fullness of your stomach tells your body to stop eating and that there are detectors in the stomach wall that respond to the presence of food, particularly the weight of food in the stomach. Experiments with animals have shown that when food is injected directly into the stomach and the smell and taste of food is missing, the animals will not eat afterwards, showing that their hunger had been satisfied. Experiments have also shown how precisely the stomach can tell how much food has been eaten. Animals were fed, and following this a measured amount of food was withdrawn from the stomach. When allowed to eat again, the animals ate almost exactly the same amount of food as that taken out of their stomach. This is important for bulimics to remember, because your body will strive to replace any food that is purged through this mechanism of detection, leading to a binge–purge cycle that continually upsets your body's physiological hunger-satiation mechanisms. You cannot fool your body as to what you are eating or purging!

Which foods? Sensing your body's needs

Your body also detects what sort of food you are eating and the chemical nature of the nutrients. In nature, carnivorous animals automatically hunt prey in such a way that the nutritional gains exceed the energy used in catching their food. It wouldn't make sense in terms of survival of the fittest to spend more energy hunting prey than you gain from eating it. Similarly, herbivores graze the appropriate amount of food for the nutritional requirements of their bodies. In other words, animals know by physiological feedback mechanisms the nutritional value of their food, and hunt, forage and eat accordingly. And although in the modern world of junk food we seem to have lost touch with these built-in sensors, they are there and have served us well through the millions of years of human evolution. If we can learn to listen to the needs of our bodies we can gain optimum nutrition and health.

Nutrient-dense food will satisfy hunger more quickly than nutrient-poor food. Animals that eat grass, which is relatively nutrient-poor, have to eat huge quantities to gain the correct nutrition, whereas animals such as lions or other predators that eat nutrient-dense food need much less to satisfy their nutritional requirements.

The human need for nutrient-dense foods

Our own physiological mechanisms also work this way. You might find it impossible to binge on meat, for example, but it is easy to over-indulge in ice cream or cake. That is because your satiation mechanism tells you after a certain amount of meat has been eaten that your nutritional requirements have been met and that you can stop eating. But when you eat processed and junk food, it is so poor in nutrients that you need a huge amount to get any nutrition from it. It is loaded with empty calories that are subsequently stored as fat.

This is the main cause of obesity in the modern world. If we ate natural nutrient-dense foods we would gradually and naturally eat less at each meal and also adjust to a lower food intake over time. Compulsive eaters override this natural instinct and continue to eat after they have satisfied their hunger, leading to weight gain when the excess food is stored in fat cells.

Social and cultural habits

Besides the physiological need to eat, we often eat according to cultural and social habits. Most Europeans eat three meals a day at around the same time of day, feeling hunger at about the right time and eating about the same amount of food at each meal. But this habit is not biologically determined; it is mostly determined by habit and by cultural norms. If you miss a meal you will generally feel hungry, but this feeling, rather than growing as you might expect if it were biologically determined, will subside by the time you would normally have eaten the meal, and then grow again by the next mealtime. In other words, hunger can respond to a learned pattern.

Another socially and culturally derived habit is what we eat. The accepted foods of societies other than our own may be distasteful to us and vice versa. It is simply a matter of learned habits and practices.

Social situations also encourage us to participate in eating; to eat when we are not physiologically hungry and to overeat. If everyone else at the party is eating, it is very difficult not to join them. In the Western world, our regular eating habits mean that we rarely experience a substantial feeling of hunger.

Social and cultural habits, rituals and practices are some of the most difficult areas for compulsive eaters to get to grips with, and frequently lead to social withdrawal. It is important that we have strategies in place for dealing with social and cultural pressures to eat when we do not need or want to. We will look at this later in the book.

4

The consequences of compulsive overeating and bulimia

Physical consequences

The physical effects of a binge can be extremely uncomfortable, as overeaters know all too well, producing abdominal bloating and discomfort. In extreme cases, the stomach can be damaged or even tear. Fullness leads to breathlessness because the distended stomach pushes up against the diaphragm. General digestive problems are common, including stomach cramps, constipation, diarrhoea, acid reflux and heartburn.

More specific problems may develop due to the nature of the food being eaten. Overeating usually involves overeating unhealthy foods. Rarely do compulsive eaters overeat meat, fish or fresh vegetables. The sort of food included in a binge is often starchy foods such as bread, pastas and cereals, salty snacks such as crisps and nuts or sugary foods such as chocolate, cakes, ice cream and sweets. This leads to problems with insulin secretion and insulin sensitivity, and overloads our bodies with processed carbohydrates.

Insulin, the 'fat hormone'

Insulin is a very powerful hormone with a major role in weight control. It is known as the 'fat hormone' because of the importance it has in controlling the use and storage of energy and converting excess glucose into the fat stores on your body. Because it is such a vital component in the problems of obesity and weight control it is worth reviewing how the insulin mechanism works in our bodies.

When you eat a meal, it is digested in the stomach and small intestine. The fat is broken down into fatty acids, the protein is broken down into amino acids, and the body uses these for energy and other functions in the body such as the repair of tissues. Carbohydrates are broken down into simple sugars that quickly and easily become glucose, the easiest form of energy our body can use. Therefore carbohydrates converted to glucose are the first and immediate form of fuel the body uses. As more carbohydrate is eaten and absorbed into the bloodstream as glucose, the blood glucose level rises. This is potentially dangerous for the body and so a feedback mechanism kicks in: the release of insulin from the pancreas. Insulin mops up the glucose that is not needed immediately for energy and converts it into glycogen, which is then transported to the liver and muscles as a short-term energy store for when the blood glucose begins to fall. The important thing to remember is that once the storage area in the liver and muscles is full, insulin converts the excess glucose to fat and stores it in your fat cells.

As we saw previously, there are processed and unprocessed carbohydrates. The unprocessed type are the complex, long-acting type that our bodies have evolved to cope with, and so insulin does an efficient job of organizing these forms of sugar into energy storage. However, the modern processed sugars, such as those found in cakes, sweets, pastries, doughnuts, jams, and a host of other modern sugary and starchy foods, raise blood glucose levels far too quickly and dramatically, causing an overload and an overstimulation of insulin production in the pancreas (within the groups of cells known as the islets of Langerhans). This causes too much glucose to be mopped up by the excess insulin and the blood glucose levels fall too low, a condition familiar to diabetics and known as hypoglycaemia. The physical symptoms include fatigue, shakiness, headaches, confusion and ultimately coma. This slump in blood glucose causes a reaction in the body as it tries to adjust the blood glucose levels to within normal limits. Hormones such as adrenaline are released to try to raise glucose levels again. This balancing act between the release of insulin and countermeasures to liberate glucose from storage happens automatically, although the unnatural situation, caused by too many refined sugars in the diet, can lead to problems with our bodies since they evolved to cope with natural foods, not modern sugar-rich foods. The finely tuned mechanism that balances blood glucose and keeps it within normal limits can become unstable and lead to imbalances in blood glucose levels and eventually diabetes. The protein and fat in our foods do not require the production of insulin at all, or at least in very small quantities, so eating these does not elicit the insulin response. It is refined and processed carbohydrates in the modern diet that cause problems.

Hyperinsulinism

When the body is continually being bombarded with high levels of refined sugar, the body produces too much insulin since there is a glut of glucose that needs to be transported to the storage areas in the liver and fat cells. Over time, the cells in the body that need glucose for energy become less sensitive to insulin – in other words, they become insulin resistant. This causes tiredness and lethargy in obese people and leads to a condition known as hyperinsulinism, in which more and more glucose is converted to fat in an effort to keep the blood glucose below danger levels. It becomes increasingly difficult to lose weight. Type II diabetes often follows. Other conditions which are linked to hyperinsulinism include high blood pressure, heart disease due to the formation of plaques in the arteries, and the increased risk of certain cancers. This syndrome of conditions related to insulin resistance is also known as Syndrome X.

The only way to deal with the problems of increased insulin production, insulin resistance and hyperinsulinism is to control your intake of refined carbohydrates. Stop eating refined sugar altogether and limit your intake of certain carbohydrates until your insulin levels are back to normal. Give your body a rest from sugar!

The secret to losing weight is through carbohydrates and insulin production. When you reduce your carbohydrate intake, you decrease your insulin production so glucose is not stored as fat. When your glycogen energy stores in the liver and muscle are used up, your body begins to break down fat to use for energy and you lose weight.

If you want to prove this to yourself, eat nothing but fat and protein for a few days and you will see a dramatic weight loss, even when you eat more calories than you would if you ate carbohydrates. I am not recommending this as a long-term diet, but if you need proof, it illustrates how important insulin is as 'the fat hormone'.

Diabetes

There are two types of diabetes: type I, or juvenile onset diabetes, affects children of around 8–12 years of age. It presents with a sudden onset of symptoms, such as sudden weight loss and insatiable thirst, and is caused by a failure of the islets of Langerhans in the pancreas to produce insulin. People with type I diabetes need insulin injections to control their blood sugar levels.

However, the vast majority of diabetics have type II diabetes, which can be controlled by diet or oral medication (see the title by Susan Elliot-Wright in Further reading). Type II diabetes is also known as mature onset diabetes. It is often found in overweight people and can occur at any period of life, although the risk increases with age. It is more common in inactive people and those who take little exercise. Controlling carbohydrate intake can prevent mature onset diabetes caused by hyperinsulinism.

Vomiting

Vomiting is the forceful expulsion of food from the upper gastrointestinal tract through the mouth. It is a reflex coordinated by the vomiting centre in the brain, a region of the brain stem. Neural inputs from several areas of the body can stimulate the vomiting reflex, for example the excessive distension of the stomach or small intestine, various substances such as salt water or poison acting on receptors in the intestinal wall, increased pressure within the skull, movements of the head such as motion sickness, intense pain in the body and stimulation to the gag reflex at the back of the throat. Excessive vomiting can lead to large losses of fluids and salts, resulting in dehydration and a disturbed salt balance that can in turn cause circulatory problems due to a reduction in extracellular fluid (plasma volume). Vomiting can also alter the acid–alkaline balance of the body, lowering acidity to unhealthy levels.

Repeated self-induced vomiting as a method of compensating for overeating can have a number of adverse effects and medical problems. It causes the irreversible erosion of dental enamel due to prolonged contact with hydrochloric acid from the stomach. Brushing the teeth after vomiting actually exacerbates this damage, although many people continue to do it. Vomiting also causes the salivary glands at the sides of the jaw to swell, causing discomfort and puffiness around the face, and often there is damage to the throat from stimulating the vomiting reflex. Fluid and electrolyte imbalances are common, and a low sodium level can result in irregularities in the heartbeat. Acid reflux can also occur through the weakening of the oesophageal sphincter at the base of the oesophagus causing the stomach contents to spill back up the oesophagus. This can lead to choking as well as irritation of the lining of the oesophagus, and can result in oesophageal ulcers that can eventually bleed and/or rupture. Rarely but significantly, there are serious medical complications with repeated vomiting, such as tears to the stomach or oesophagus, that constitute a medical emergency.

Bulimics frequently use vomiting as a method of compensating for compulsive overeating and a way to regain control over their eating. However, as a method of compensating for large amounts of calories consumed, it is not very effective because many of the calories are absorbed in the stomach and intestine by the time the binge is finished, and vomiting subsequently leads to feelings of hunger some time later so that the cycle of bingeing and purging continues.

Misuse of laxatives

Although some people who overeat try to compensate for the calories consumed by using laxatives, alone or as an additional measure to vomiting, they are completely ineffective since they have no effect on the absorption of calories from the stomach and intestines. Any weight loss effect is through water loss from the bowel due to diarrhoea and has no effect on fat loss. People can develop a tolerance to laxatives and the bowel effectively becomes lazy. This leads to constipation once the laxatives are stopped. Also, the body will tend to retain water as a countermeasure to losing water in the faeces, and puffiness and oedema can result. Laxatives are sometimes used as a form of self-punishment because of the unpleasant side effects, although this approach is very unhelpful.

Diuretics

Pills that are used to remove excess water, as with laxatives, have a temporary effect on body weight and are of little use in a weight-loss plan or to control unhealthy eating habits.

Diet pills

Any drug that professes to help you lose weight is unhelpful and many of these medications can be dangerous and addictive. They are primarily designed to make money for the manufacturer. Taking diet pills does nothing to help you develop healthy eating habits or to understand the problem of compulsive overeating, and most drugs of this type carry contraindications for anyone with an eating disorder. They should be avoided at all costs unless prescribed by your doctor following a proper consultation.

Excessive exercise

Although exercise has many wonderful health benefits and should be encouraged, it is ineffective when used as the sole means of losing weight. To lose a single pound of body weight you would have to use up 3,500 calories, which is a walk of about 50 miles. Some compulsive eaters overexercise as a means of compensating for the extra calories consumed, but in reality this cannot work.

Psychological consequences

One of the psychological consequences of compulsive overeating is that food takes over your life. Your thoughts are constantly preoccupied with food, your weight and body image, and as a result depression, anxiety and isolation can have a profound effect on the life of a compulsive eater or bulimic. Social interactions can suffer – some people withdraw completely from social activity when they feel out of control. Compulsive eating is largely a secret activity and can be very isolating and lonely. It does not help the situation when social interactions so frequently revolve around eating and drinking at parties, meals in restaurants and family get-togethers around the dinner table. For a compulsive eater or bulimic, these events are unsettling, difficult or even frightening in some cases. It is often easier to avoid them altogether, so that it is possible to end up cut off from an ordinary social life, or at least limited in time spent with other people in a social situation. Family relationships with partners and children can also become strained and difficult around mealtimes and are a source of anxiety.

However, the feelings of shame, anxiety, depression and worthlessness are a consequence of compulsive eating and bulimia. Often when the disorder is brought under control these symptoms subside. Even panic attacks and severe anxiety can be controlled when eating problems are addressed. Depression, feelings of hopelessness, guilt and social withdrawal are relieved in the majority of cases once the problems with compulsive eating and bulimia are overcome. This suggests that psychological problems, far from being the cause of compulsive eating, are in fact a consequence of it, and so a physical cause should be sought as a priority. This book aims to do just that.

5

A natural diet

This chapter is crucial, and fundamental to our understanding of why we may develop compulsive eating and bulimia. Our bodies are not designed to cope with the daily onslaught of modern food to which we subject them, and by looking at our ancestry we can begin to understand why this is so.

What our human ancestors ate

Around 3.75 to 3.2 million years ago, an ancestor of modern humans – *Australopithecus aferensis*, also known as 'Lucy' – was to be found in Africa. Lucy walked upright and ate a traditional primate diet of fruit and vegetation, insects and possibly small animals. The diet was varied, with more than 300 different species of plants, insects and animals on the menu. These provided a diet rich in protein and nutrient-dense foods, including fat. The early human digestive tract and dentition had become adapted to this diet over millions of years of primate evolution.

About 2.5 to 2 million years ago, during the Palaeolithic era, *Homo habilis* (or 'handy man') was to be found in Africa, and it appears that this early human ancestor used primitive tools to scrape and cut meat from animals that were scavenged, and to break bones and skulls in order to obtain bone marrow and the brains of animals killed by predators such as lions. The addition of more meat and protein to the diet was instrumental in allowing the large brain of our human ancestors to develop and triple in size. The scavenged brains would have been particularly nutritious since they contain an omega-3 fat called docosahexaenoic acid, DHA, which is the building block of our brain tissue. Without this, the human brain would not have expanded and we would not have become the sophisticated animals we are today.

Later, around 1.8 to 1.6 million years ago, *Homo erectus* appeared in the fossil record of human ancestry. Also called 'Java man', he had the largest brain yet of the human or primate lineage and used up to 25 per cent of his daily calorie intake to fuel this brain (monkeys use just 8 per cent). His diet included not only scavenged meat, killed by other animals, for *H. erectus* also actively hunted wild animals for meat. *H. erectus* was so successful that he outlived all other humanlike species on Earth at that time, surviving until around 300,000 years ago.

Ancestral humans ate the most varied diet of any primate, and it was probably the most nutritious diet of any animal on Earth. It was so successful that there began to be a division of labour among humans, women gathering fruit, leaves, nuts and wild plants while the men hunted animals and continued to scavenge meat.

Homo sapiens

Between 500,000 and 180,000 years ago, *Homo sapiens*, or archaic humans, gradually replaced *H. erectus* and lived alongside other early humans such as *Homo neanderthalensis*, or Neanderthals as they have become known. *H. sapiens* lived in communities and were very social, bringing food back to a home area rather than roaming the countryside. They had mental maps of the best places to find food and hunt animals and had created special killing areas where they drove large prey, often over cliffs, so that they would fall to their deaths and provide huge amounts of meat for the whole community. The human population began to grow and early humans began to share and barter for food and other provisions, possible because of the great variety of food they ate in their diet. Humans began to settle into a more sedentary lifestyle. By 30,000 years ago, other human ancestors, such as *H. neanderthalensis*, died out and left *H. sapiens* as the lone humans on Earth.

Our own species, *Homo sapiens sapiens*, evolved by 40,000 years ago during the Stone Age or Neolithic period. They looked almost exactly as we do now, except they were taller, leaner and fitter and had barely any signs at all of tooth decay (just two per cent of fossil teeth show decay). They continued to forage for vegetation, fruit and nuts and hunt wild animals for meat as their ancestors had done. As time went on the human population grew, the wild animals they had hunted became extinct and Stone Age man, for one reason or another, began to grow food from seeds and store it for use during the harsh winter. By about 10,000 years ago they had begun to keep wild animals as pets and use them for food, and the road to domestication of animals and plants began, changing the diet of humans as never before. Within about four to six generations, just 200–300 years, man had cultivated three of the seven core grains, which were chosen not because of their nutritional value but because they were easy to grow, harvest and store.

The Agricultural Revolution

Around 12,000–10,000 years ago, hunter-gatherers became farmers. The Agricultural Revolution occurred. Cereal grains were adopted as a staple diet and animals became domesticated. This is a mere 500 generations ago, barely enough time for genetic changes to keep pace. In the natural world, evolutionary adaptations take millions of years to evolve and yet humans, with our large brain and higher intelligence, have fast-forwarded our cultural evolution. However, our genetic makeup and our physical bodies have not had a chance to catch up. Our bodies are trying to cope with a diet of modern foods they are not adequately evolved to cope with. As a result, it is believed that this is why humans are suffering the so-called diseases of civilization, including obesity, heart disease, hypertension, diabetes, cancer, food allergies, food intolerances – and compulsive overeating and bulimia.

Before Stone Age man began to domesticate and cultivate his food, hunter-gatherers obtained about 30–35 per cent of their nutrition from animals and the other 65–70 per cent from plants. We know what they ate from archaeological and fossil evidence, the analysis of the nutritional values found in wild plants and animals, and by studying the few modern hunter-gatherer tribes left. Fossils show the type of teeth and the patterns of wear our ancestors had, from which an analysis of their diet can be made. Fossilized pollen found around archaeological sites can show what plants were once found there. Analysis of the proteins in preserved hair can identify the diet that was eaten, while the many and varied stone tools found at sites give other valuable clues as to the diet of our ancestors.

They ate a huge variety of wild plants (there are up to 100,000 edible wild plants on Earth), and although some 3,000 were used as food, only 150 plant species were cultivated. Now we live on fewer than 20 main crops, such as maize, wheat, barley and oats. And while the early farmers cultivated wild grains, modern processing only uses the inner starchy endosperm of the grain, which is devoid of nutrients and fibre. The few vitamins and minerals they do have actually disrupt the metabolism of bone minerals such as vitamin D and calcium in our bodies, leading to diseases such as rickets and osteoporosis where grains are the main source of calories in underdeveloped countries. Processed grains contain little goodness and so few vitamins and minerals that manufacturers have to fortify cereals and breads with them. Fortifying food should not be necessary and it certainly isn't when you eat wholesome natural unprocessed foods. Furthermore, cereals even contain chemicals known as antinutrients, which actually prevent nutrients being absorbed, causing diseases of the gastrointestinal tract. Starch from grains is mixed with fat, sugar and salt to produce a host of convenience foods with a very high calorie content. The only variety we get in our modern diet is how many different ways we can eat processed grains, such as in crackers, noodles, pastas, bread and biscuits. Even 'wholemeal' and 'wholegrain' flours may be unhealthy. Granted they may be marginally better than highly processed white flour, but they still have a high glycaemic index and can contribute to diet-related diseases, including obesity and compulsive overeating. Grains are not necessarily good for your health; they are simply a cheap way to mass-produce food.

Phytochemicals

Natural unprocessed foods are full of vitamins, minerals and phytochemicals. Phytochemicals are compounds that prevent cancer, protect against ageing and heart disease and probably boost the immune system. Our ancestors must have eaten large quantities of these phytochemicals, yet on the levels of fresh fruit and vegetables we eat, we are barely getting a third of the phytochemicals our bodies need for healthy functioning.

Wild animals

Our ancestors also ate a huge variety of wild animals; now we have just a few domesticated species that we routinely eat. Instead of the diverse diet of our predecessors, modern humans subsist on a poor selection of overprocessed food and domesticated meat full of fat because the animals are sedentary and fed on cereal-based diets, pumped full of antibiotics and other chemicals that were not present in the wild animals that were hunted just 500 generations ago. Often we do not eat the natural cuts of meat but derivatives of it such as beefburgers, hamburgers, hot dogs and corned beef that are padded out with processed starch.

Sugar

Sugar is the scourge of the modern diet. Refined sugar (sucrose) was unheard of until some 200 years ago and is another major player in the catalogue of diet-related diseases in modern humans. Modern man eats a staggering 30–40 teaspoons of refined sugar every day! Sugar is found not only in the obvious foods such as sweets, sugary drinks, biscuits and cakes but also hidden in baked beans, sauces, flavoured yoghurts, cereals and many, many other processed foods. Refined sugar is off the scale as a high glycaemic index food and is responsible for much of the obesity and chronic disease that is such an intractable problem in society today. We also have a real problem with tooth decay that our ancestors didn't have to worry about. Tooth decay has gone up from two per cent in Stone Age man to 95 per cent in modern man, thanks to our sugary diet. We probably eat more sugar in a day than our ancestors ate in their whole lives!

The problems of agriculture

We may be able to produce larger quantities of food per acre of land thanks to agriculture, but we have lost the amazing diversity in our diet that allowed humans to become large-brained intelligent creatures in the first place. Modern humans are effectively suffering from malnutrition. During the post-Agricultural Revolution, this relatively poor nutrition caused health defects such as vitamin and mineral deficiencies, which we still see today. Diseases such as beriberi and vitamin B deficiencies became common and persisted into the 1800s until the cause was isolated as a nutritional deficiency. Blindness and skin conditions developed because of a lack of dark leafy vegetables and liver that provided vitamin A in abundance in the hunter-gatherer diet. Rickets developed because of a lack of vitamin D. Tooth decay was rare prior to agriculture but became rife, along with anaemia, brittle bones and stunted growth. Height dropped by about four to six inches on average, a good indicator of nutritional status. Infectious diseases such as typhus, smallpox, tuberculosis, bubonic plague and measles spread and the human immune system was suppressed because of poor nutrition and the close proximity and poor sanitation of people living in large communities. The unique characteristic of the human species, a large brain, also suffered because of agriculture and the poor nutrition that resulted from it. Brain size began to decrease and even today, the average brain of a human is around 11 per cent smaller that those of our ancestors prior to the advent of agriculture.

There were many other problems caused by agriculture. The need for labour on the farm meant that more children were born to provide help. They were also weaned earlier to allow mothers to work on the farm and because children were born closer together. Prior to agriculture, babies were breast fed for years, but early weaning suddenly deprived children of vital nutrition in their developing years. Infant mortality increased, and because bones were so brittle owing to a lack of calcium, malformations of the pelvis were common in women. This was such a problem that it was advocated by medical doctors in the 1880s that pregnant women deliberately retard the growth of their babies by restricting calories and fluids to make birth easier when there were bone problems.

Prior to agriculture, the human population on Earth was around five to ten million, but farming unleashed a human population explosion – an exponential increase in human numbers that has ultimately led to the problems encountered today by squeezing six billion people on to the planet. More and more land was turned over to farming, which subsequently destroyed the natural habitat and the lifestyle of our pre-agriculture ancestors for ever.

The Industrial Revolution and afterwards

In the late eighteenth and early nineteenth centuries, the Industrial Revolution further changed human lives by the mechanization of farming, which reduced the need for physical activity. Labour-saving transport and equipment has reduced calorie expenditure in humans by over 60 per cent. We are sedentary in the extreme when compared to our early ancestors. Following the Industrial Revolution, we were able to refine sugar and flour, transport food and develop food-processing techniques such as canning, which led to further refinements in our diet. By the mid-twentieth century, food processing included modified fats, and this, combined with the variety of additives, colouring agents, emulsifiers and preservatives, gave us the mind-boggling array of processed foods we see today.

In the 1950s, saturated fats were linked to heart disease, high blood cholesterol and hypertension. Unfortunately, red meat was wrongly implicated as unhealthy and became a scapegoat for heart disease and bowel cancer. So called 'healthy alternatives' were developed, such as polyunsaturated margarines and vegetable oils, but we now know that these polyunsaturated fats contain high levels of omega-6 fatty acids at the expense of the healthy omega-3 fatty acids. The use of these margarines and spreads introduced trans-fatty acids into our diet, which was very bad news indeed. Following this, another big mistake in the nutritional guidelines was replacing saturated fats with starchy carbohydrates such as bread, cereals and potatoes. Now, the glycaemic index is a measure of how different carbohydrates affect blood glucose levels. Low glycaemic carbohydrates, which include natural carbohydrates such as fruit and vegetables, are good for our health and cause a minimal or slow rise in blood glucose. The high glycaemic index carbohydrates, such as refined and processed sugars and starches, cause a rapid increase in blood glucose and contribute to diseases such as Syndrome X, which includes mature onset diabetes, insulin resistance, hypertension, heart disease, obesity and high LDL (low density lipoproteins) cholesterol levels ('bad' cholesterol).

The results today

Today we eat too little protein (in fact only half the amount our ancestors ate); too many processed foods and high glycaemic index refined carbohydrates instead of natural carbohydrates such as fruit and vegetables; not enough fibre in the form of fresh fruit and vegetables; and too much of the wrong sort of fat and not enough of the good sort (omega-3 fats are the good sort). We also take in too much salt and not enough potassium. Our ancestors ate a diet rich in potassium and low in sodium (up to ten times as much potassium as sodium). Salt was probably introduced with farming as a preservative for meat and other food. Now our salty diet gives us twice as much sodium as potassium, which is unhealthy. The acid–alkaline balance of our diet has also been altered, and this can affect our health. Our ancestors ate lots of fresh fruit and vegetables, which are alkaline, and lots of meat and fish, which are acid. This balanced out and was the correct acid–alkaline base for our bodies. Now, however, we eat too many acidic foods, such as dairy and salty foods, and not enough alkaline foods, causing a shift in the acid–alkaline base towards acid. This acidity causes hypertension, the risk of kidney stones, bone and muscle loss as we age as well as the exacerbation of asthma.

In terms of evolution, there has been virtually no time for our bodies to adjust to the radical changes in our diet. Our genetic makeup is more than 99 per cent identical to that of our primate ancestors before humans and 99.9 per cent of our genes are identical to our human ancestors of 10,000 years ago. In fact the human genome has changed less than 0.02 per cent in the past 40,000 years. For 100,000 generations humans lived on wild foods, gathering vegetation, fruit, nuts and seeds as well as scavenging and later hunting wild animals. Since the advent of agriculture, people have been farming and growing their own food for just 500 generations, and since the Industrial Revolution, when mechanization saw an explosion in food processing, it has been just ten generations. Computers have been around for one generation, yet our bodies are still genetically adapted to the diet of wild food eaten by our human ancestors some 10,000 years ago.

The quality of modern life has certainly improved from that of our ancestors in certain respects: improved sanitation, medicine, science and technology are able to overcome diseases, reduce infant mortality and lengthen lifespan considerably. But the diseases of civilization are still generally a modern phenomenon: some 70 per cent of cancers and more than 50 per cent of heart disease are caused by diet and lifestyle. Obesity is on the increase, is reaching crisis proportions and is undoubtedly linked to an unsuitable diet and an inactive lifestyle. Food intolerance and gastrointestinal disorders from minor indigestion to serious conditions like bowel cancers are all too common and are known to be linked to diet and lifestyle.

Stone Age man undoubtedly had his share of health problems, and living wild can be a dangerous occupation with the constant fear of becoming prey to wild animals. However, we can make comparisons when we look at the few modern populations of hunter-gatherers that are left in the world and even people in modern societies who eat lots of fruit and vegetables. These people rarely suffer from heart disease, cancers, diabetes, stroke or hypertension. They also have lower rates of depression, anxiety or suicide, and obesity is unheard of. They stay lean and fit with no loss of memory or mental ability as they age. Yet when these people are brought into a modern society and adopt a modern diet, their physical and mental health and well-being begins to deteriorate and they develop these conditions within just one or two generations. We also know that ancient humans were strong, lean and fit.

The trend towards fortifying modern food with vitamins, minerals and phytochemicals may appear to be a good thing, but in reality we know so little about the interactions of these chemicals, the correct doses and the long-term effects that we are making dangerous assumptions. We have been eating genetically altered foods for some time now and there is a trend towards high-tech food and dietary supplements designed to boost energy, enhance mood, reduce appetite, improve mental ability – the list goes on. When you think of the way current opinion concerning nutrition can change in the light of new evidence (such as the issue of polyunsaturated fats), and the way fads and fashions in nutrition and dietary supplementation change over time, it would be foolish to rely on any new trends led by manufacturers who add health-enhancing compounds to our food, particularly when profit is really at the heart of food production for manufacturers. Competition for consumers' money leads to ever more extravagant claims that a particular food will magically provide us with the nutrition we need. Even government guidelines on diet change along with the drifting opinion of medicine and science. This is inevitable since scientific studies are continually revealing more about our physiology. Conflicting evidence does little to reassure us that the latest study is anything but another piece of knowledge to add to the jigsaw. Don't be carried away by the latest trends in nutrition and medicine. What is best for our bodies and what we need to keep us healthy is the natural diet our genetic makeup has evolved and adapted to use. Our bodies are highly complex and intricate biological mechanisms that have worked extremely well for millions of years, making our species the most successful on Earth. Surely the diet that has sustained us all this time and allowed our large brain and intelligence to develop is the best one for us; not the chemical concoctions characteristic of modern food.

So what has all this got to do with compulsive overeating and bulimia? Well, when we eat a diet that is unsuitable for our bodies we develop food intolerances and food sensitivities (these are distinct from food allergies that are serious medical emergencies and that can be life threatening). We will look at these further, but for now, we need to understand why diets don't work.

6

Why diets don't work

A weight-loss diet is defined as a regime of eating whereby we eat fewer calories than we need, so breaking down body fat to use as energy. Whether you opt for counting calories, or go on the latest fad diet, you are depriving your body of the variety of nutrients it needs and it will do everything it can to make up that deficit in order to preserve your energy, your health and even your life.

Because of our normal physiology, weight-loss diets cause you to put on more weight in the long term. In fact 95–98 per cent of people who lose weight by reducing calories by whatever method end up regaining the weight lost and putting on more for good measure. This is inevitable when you consider how the physiology of the human body works and how we evolved to deal with food shortages, which is exactly what a reducing diet is – a food shortage.

Our Stone Age ancestors were forced to endure famines when food was in short supply. A layer of fat was a survival mechanism that provided energy during these enforced fasts. People with little fat, perhaps coupled with a high metabolism, couldn't survive these fasts and so died out, leaving the successful humans as the ones who could adapt to fasting by developing fat stores during times of plenty and being able to lower their metabolism in order to use less energy when food was in short supply. We have evolved to use our body fat to survive.

Our ancient ancestors found it hard to get enough fat or sugar in their diet, so they didn't develop a mechanism that stopped them eating too much fat or sugar; there was no need for one. They ate all they could get in the form of meat and fruit, with the occasional seasonal treat of honey, and their bodies stored any excess as energy stores of body fat. Obesity was unheard of in our ancient ancestors. Women needed extra fat storage capacity to see them through the extra demands on their bodies from pregnancy, so it is easy to see why women put on weight more easily and why it is harder to shift it. Our bodies are very efficient at storing fat and absorb around 95 per cent of the fat from our food intake, while almost 100 per cent of the sugar is absorbed. So our bodies have evolved to be highly efficient at fat storage; in fact we have evolved many mechanisms in the body that are designed to encourage weight gain and prevent weight loss. Our bodies have not yet learned to cope with a modern diet or learned to compensate for the high calorie food we eat, so obesity continues to rise.

When we diet we initiate this ancient natural survival mechanism and it resets our metabolism at a lower level in order to protect our fat stores. When the famine or diet is over, and we start eating more food again, our bodies increase our fat stores and add a bit extra for good measure in readiness for the next famine. Thus a cycle of yo-yo dieting becomes established.

When we diet by cutting calories or skipping meals we crave food. When we restrict the amount or variety of foods we eat, such as when we follow fad diets, we also experience cravings, which is another ancient inbuilt mechanism designed to give us all the nutrients we need from various foods in order to stay healthy.

Our hunger and satiation sensors in our stomach still tell us when we have eaten enough, by the weight of food and the feeling of fullness in our stomach, but instead of pounds of low-calorie healthy vegetables, we are filling our stomachs with high-calorie refined foods. Pound for pound (nearly half a kilogram), you could either eat a pound of vegetables for about 100 calories or a pound of chocolate cake for 2,500 calories. Either way you satisfy your hunger but our bodies can also detect the chemicals and substances contained in the food we eat. We are satisfied with less of the healthy nutrient-dense foods since these are packed full of the correct nutrients our bodies need. Refined and processed foods, however, are full of calories but short of nutrients, so our body requires more and more of these foods in order to get enough nutrition. The result is that we overeat refined high-calorie foods and become overweight. When you overeat compulsively on processed foods you are responding not only to likely food intolerances but also to your body's need for nutrition.

Another problem with dieting is that once the body uses up its fuel reserves, it will start to break down muscle tissue as well as fat. Muscle boosts the metabolic rate and uses more calories than fat, and so when you lose muscle you also lower your metabolism, making it even harder to lose weight. People who are continuously on a diet end up having more fat than muscle and every time they regain weight after a diet they just get fatter and fatter and it becomes increasingly hard to lose weight. The more muscle mass you have the higher your metabolism, which results in more calories being used as energy even at rest. You can increase muscle mass with weight-bearing exercises, and we will look at this further later on.

Popular weight-loss diets

Slimming groups such as Weight Watchers or Slimming World provide moral support and encouragement for those on a diet, but there is no real evidence that these groups are able to achieve long-term weight loss in their clients. They are still advocating a reduction in either calories or major food groups, which does not work in the long term and leads to yo-yo dieting and a cycle of bingeing and starving. Many members of these groups seem to be permanent fixtures – people who return time and time again, year after year, because they have regained the weight they had lost and believe that it is somehow their fault for having relapsed. They believe that 'this time it will be different'. A radical new approach is needed, not simply repeating the same weight-loss programme over and over again.

Fad diets are usually followed by fans of the celebrities who promote them. They frequently advocate nutritionally unsound diets with no concern for scientific evidence, and like counting calories or restricting food groups, these diets have no prospects for long-term weight loss and many can be harmful if followed for prolonged periods. New diets are continually being promoted and the diet industry makes billions of pounds and dollars every year. Fad diets are simply money-making projects, and logic suggests that these diets do not work in the long term.

Low-fat diets, popular in the 1980s and 1990s, advocated diets low in fat and high in carbohydrates. The belief at the time was that dietary fat caused obesity but they failed to realize the importance of essential fats for our health. Low-fat diets also led dieters to overeat carbohydrates, and as we have seen throughout this book, this is the worst thing you can do for your health and your figure.

Low carbohydrate diets such as the Atkins diet, a concept promoted by Dr Robert Atkins, advocated a high protein and fat intake while reducing carbohydrates. While this diet undoubtedly works as a temporary weight-loss method, it is unsustainable over the long term and the carbohydrate restrictions are too severe for most people, making it unsustainable. Again, with this diet, once you begin to increase your carbohydrate intake, the lost weight is soon regained, making it another diet that doesn't work over the long term. Another problem with the Atkins diet is that high levels of fatty meat, cheese, butter and cream are encouraged, with only small amounts of vegetables and little or no fruit. This diet is too high in saturated fat, with far too little fruit and vegetables, and is not the natural diet we should be eating if we are to work in harmony with our bodies.

Vegetarian diets can be healthy diets providing plenty of fresh fruit and vegetables are eaten and there is sufficient protein in the diet to replace the protein that would normally be obtained from meat. Also, it is important to avoid refined carbohydrates, as with any other long-term diet, since the risks of overloading the body with processed foods is as much of a risk for vegetarians as for carnivores.

Very low calorie diets, such as those offering replacement meals in the form of milkshakes, etc., can be very unhealthy if followed for long periods, and may cause vitamin and mineral imbalances. These complex nutrients are still poorly understood and it is risky to replace natural foods with chemicals. As with all diets that restrict calories or food groups, the metabolism will reset itself at a lower level and the body will go into starvation mode, making weight gain inevitable once the diet ends.

Apart from constant hunger, extreme dieting can also cause depression, lowered libido, fatigue, irritability, anxiety, fainting and dizziness, weakness, muscle loss, low resting metabolic rate, acidosis, and it can lead to compulsive overeating, bulimia and other eating disorders. Ultimately, it leads to increased weight gain and a cycle of dieting and bingeing.

Stop dieting!

The answer to the problems caused by reducing food intake and counting calories is to stop dieting and eat the correct food that your body needs without counting calories. This not only stops your body going into survival mode to preserve fat, but your metabolism will tick over at a higher rate and your muscle tissue will be preserved. You will be helping your physiology to operate smoothly and your body to be energy efficient, allowing you to attain the correct weight naturally and effortlessly. It is what you eat, not how much, that matters when it comes to losing weight.

Part 2

CREATING YOUR PERSONAL LIFETIME PLAN

7

Find your triggers for overeating

People tend to have specific triggers that set off an overeating episode. These may be physical triggers, or psychological ones. Both are important, although as I have stressed, it's also vital not to assume that it is 'all in the mind' or to blame oneself or one's 'lack of will-power'. Do read the physical triggers first, and give them some attention as you're working out what may cause you personally to overeat.

Physical triggers

Cravings

We crave fatty and sweet foods as our human ancestors have always done, because these are the foods that help lay down fat deposits for converting to energy during times of famine. There are at least 50 chemicals in the brain that help to control appetite, such as serotonin and endorphins, as well as stress hormones that push us to eat fat and sugar. We also derive pleasure from these substances because of these neuro-chemicals. We may also crave fatty foods in order to obtain enough essential fatty acids for brain function and other essential body functions.

Our taste buds are programmed to pick out the best-tasting food, and our appetite naturally craves sugary and fatty food as a survival instinct. The problem is that while our ancient ancestors had very limited supplies of natural sugary and fatty foods in the form of meat, fruit and occasionally honey, we have 24-hour access to modern foods packed with processed sugar and fat, and unless we take measures to control our intake our natural drive is to eat more and more of these foods. Over 50 per cent of our average diet is in the form of refined and processed foods packed with sugar and fats.

When we restrict carbohydrates from our diet (remember that vegetables and fruits are carbohydrates too) we crave them, so restricting any food group severely will cause cravings. Food intolerances and hypoglycaemia also cause food cravings.

Food intolerance

Food intolerance causes an adverse reaction to particular foods, which causes discomfort and a catalogue of symptoms, including:

- an insatiable craving for particular foods
- bloating
- constipation
- diarrhoea
- irritable bowel syndrome
- feeling cold after eating
- indigestion and heartburn
- flatulence
- weight fluctuations and weight gain
- water retention
- headaches
- fatigue and listlessness
- exhaustion
- dizziness
- hot flushes
- trembling and faintness when hungry
- insomnia
- aching muscles
- cramp
- coated tongue
- constant thirst
- breathing problems, such as gasping for air, constant yawning or chest tightness
- anxiety, depression, moodiness and irritability.

Quite a list! And all this can be caused simply by an intolerance to the food we eat – food that our human bodies are not designed or genetically adapted to cope with.

Foods to which you are intolerant or sensitive are the ones you crave the most, and as time goes on you need more and more of the food to feel satisfied. This is also true of other addictions such as nicotine, alcohol and drugs such as heroin; you need more and more of the substance you are addicted to to get a 'high' or feel satisfied. You also become dependent on these foods. When a food is eaten on a regular daily basis, often several times per day, we can become overloaded with the addictive substance in the food and the problem is aggravated further. For example, we often eat wheat several times per day in the form of cereals and toast for breakfast, sandwiches for lunch, pastas, pizzas, crackers and more bread later in the day. Food intolerance develops with overexposure to the same substance, and then you start to experience withdrawal symptoms when you don't get it, so that food addiction sets in. You begin to need that food in order to avoid the withdrawal symptoms of insatiable craving. Food addiction leads to compulsive overeating and bulimia. Have a quick look at the list you made at the beginning and see which foods you listed as the foods you tend to overeat and the foods you couldn't live without. These could well be the foods you are intolerant to and that are causing food addictions. Typical suspects in our diet are wheat, milk and sugar. (You might like to look at the two books by Alex Gazzola listed in Further reading.)

The problem foods

Grains constituted hardly any of the diet of our ancestors for 99 per cent of our evolutionary history. It was just 10,000 years ago that the early farmers started cultivating wild grains and grasses. Before this, grasses and wild grains of any sort were starvation food; they weren't part of the normal diet of our ancestors. This indicates that grains such as wheat, oats, barley and maize could be problem foods for modern humans, and there are several known health problems associated with the gluten found in wheat, such as gluten allergies, gluten ataxia (a mental deterioration) and irritable bowel syndrome, as well as the long list of uncomfortable symptoms above.

Milk was never a part of the diet of our ancestors either. In fact they didn't eat any dairy food. It would have been impossible to milk wild animals and so dairy produce became a by-product of farming domesticated animals. Milk or lactulose intolerance is another common problem in the diet of modern humans.

Candida

The normal bacteria and flora in your gut can help digestion, and nutritionists advise taking probiotics to increase the level of good bacteria in our bowel. Problems can occur when a yeast known as *Candida albicans* grows out of control. Candida is found naturally in our gut, and although it is a parasite and serves no useful purpose, it is fairly harmless most of the time. It is the same organism that causes thrush in the mouth or vagina and skin conditions like athlete's foot. Candida can proliferate at extraordinary levels, as wine and beer makers will know, and this can cause problems with our health if an overgrowth happens in our bowel. The overconsumption of processed carbohydrates produces the perfect environment for candida to grow, as do diabetes, nutritional deficiencies and a weakened immune system. Certain medications, such as the contraceptive pill and other hormones, antibiotics or steroids, can also cause an overgrowth of candida. Symptoms include all those on our list of symptoms for food intolerance, including food cravings, with the addition of fungal infections such as thrush, athlete's foot or dandruff.

Hypoglycaemia

If you think back to our discussion of insulin, you may remember that when we eat carbohydrates the pancreas releases an appropriate amount of insulin to transport the glucose to the liver as glycogen for short-term storage of energy, and when this is full it transports it to the fat cells to be stored as triglycerides – and we put on weight.

When we eat whole natural foods such as an apple or a salad, the appropriate amount of insulin is released and the body maintains the balance of glucose and insulin without problems as it has always done throughout our evolution. We have evolved to cope with natural complex carbohydrates. But when we drink a glass of apple juice or orange juice, the pancreas produces too much insulin because one glass of fruit juice contains the equivalent of several apples or oranges. When we eat modern sugary foods, insulin release peaks dramatically as a mechanism of mopping up excess glucose that could be dangerous if left in our bloodstream. Because there is so much insulin the glucose levels drop sharply within a short time after eating, and the blood glucose becomes too low, leading to cravings to eat again. This is called hypoglycaemia, and a vicious circle can become established whereby you continually experience peaks and lows in your blood glucose levels throughout the day. This unstable blood glucose causes food cravings as well

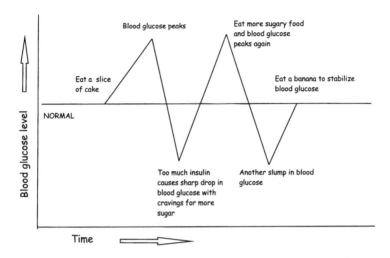

Figure 3 The hypoglycaemic cycle

as a host of other problems, such as insulin resistance and eventually diabetes. To stop the cravings associated with hypoglycaemia you need to stabilize your blood glucose, and you can only do this by controlling your carbohydrate intake. By eating a natural, long-acting, complex carbohydrate such as a banana or a salad when you experience hypoglycaemia, you begin to stabilize your blood glucose and level out your insulin production. By eating another bar of chocolate or a cream cake, you simply perpetuate the hypoglycaemic cycle (see Figure 3).

Alcohol

Just as the body craves certain foods, it can also crave alcohol. An addiction to alcohol is characterized by insatiable cravings, an increased tolerance of alcohol so that more is needed to produce the desired effect, and dependence on alcohol. Alcoholics display similar behavioural characteristics to those of compulsive over-eaters: they binge drink, they drink alone and in secret, they are socially withdrawn and may be depressed, anxious and feel shame and remorse. But why alcohol? Is it simply to get the feeling of being drunk as an escape from the world and their problems, or is it the actual ingredients in the alcohol to which an alcoholic becomes addicted? Let's explore the second option. Wine is made from grapes and the addition of yeast ferments the concentrated fruit sugar into alcohol. Beer is made from malt, hops and yeast – maltose (a sugar) is produced from the starch in the malt and fermented with the yeast. Lager is simply beer that has been stored in a dark cool place for 30 days or more. Rum is made from sugar cane, vodka is distilled from grain and sometimes potatoes, and both whisky and gin are made from grains such as barley, wheat and oats. Therefore, the key ingredients in alcohol are sugar and yeast, with either grains or concentrated fruit sugar. These ingredients are typically found in food intolerances, and Candida, as we have seen, thrives on yeast. In order to overcome the food intolerances caused by a faulty diet, we need to include alcohol as well, otherwise we will simply perpetuate the cravings for problem ingredients whether in food or alcohol.

This may also be good news for alcoholics because while the reasons for alcoholism are sometimes complex (and there is not the scope in this book to explore alcoholism), an alcoholic trying to give up drinking must also give up eating the ingredients in food that are causing addiction, such as grains, yeast and refined sugar. If alcoholism and food intolerance are tackled together, then there is a better chance of recovery for an alcoholic since he or she would be addressing all the causes of cravings and addiction. If he or she continues to eat foods containing grains, yeast and refined sugar, then the craving for alcohol will continue. Once the addiction to these ingredients is under control, along with attention to any psychological problems, it may even be possible for a former alcoholic to return to limited social drinking.

Psychological triggers

Past conditioning

From as early as four or five years of age, our personality, behaviour and preferences are well developed and form the basis of our adult personality. We carry with us throughout our lives the messages and conditioning we receive as children. While it is perfectly possible to challenge our beliefs and change the messages in our heads to ones that are more constructive in adulthood (and we will look at this later), we have first to become aware of them, since they are mostly part of our subconscious behaviour. As children:

- we are told to eat everything on our plate and not to waste food;
- we have little control over what we eat;
- we fall into the pattern of eating certain foods established by our parents or carers;
- we end up in battles about what we eat and how much we should eat;
- we eat at preordained mealtimes, not when we are hungry;
- we are conditioned to expect food treats or sweets as a reward for good behaviour, to cheer us up or as a comfort when we are upset;
- food is withheld as a form of punishment (no pudding if you don't eat your dinner; no sweets if you don't behave);
- we eat the wrong foods as a form of defiance against authority;
- we see food as a treat when we are being nice to ourselves.

When these childhood messages are emphasized strongly enough or when we are particularly susceptible or sensitive to them, behavioural conditioning can lead to issues of control around food, and ultimately to eating disorders. Once we reach adulthood we are able to choose what we eat, but sometimes we become stuck in a negative or unhealthy relationship with food and play out old conditioned behaviour such as eating to please people in social or family situations, eating for emotional comfort when we are feeling low, or withholding food from ourselves as a form of punishment. We may eat when we are happy or to celebrate an achievement and use food as a reward or treat.

Emotional overeating may stem from conditioning during childhood, especially if we were constantly rewarded or punished with food. If we are conditioned to eat every time we are upset when we are children, then it is not surprising that this behaviour continues into adulthood. There is nothing complex about it and we are not neurotic. We have simply learned to use food as a comfort. The sort of food we tend to overeat, such as ice cream, cakes, chocolate and sweets, are the same foods parents use to pacify children when they are upset or as rewards and treats for good behaviour.

In the vast majority of cases, the psychological 'problems' asso-ciated with compulsive overeating and bulimia are generally a consequence of the disorder, not a cause of it. Depression, anxiety, social withdrawal, obsession (with food), irritability, feelings of hopelessness, shame and guilt are due to the lack of control over-eaters feel they have over their condition. This set of symptoms could be present whenever a person is unhappy with aspects of their life, regardless of whether it is oriented around food. All these symptoms could be applied to someone who has lost their job, experienced a relationship break-up, lost a loved one or any number of other situations in life. They are a normal reaction to events. These symptoms are not exclusive to eating disorders or diagnostic of them, but whereas other life events come and go, problems with eating are perpetuated over long periods of time because we have to eat every day.

Once compulsive eating is under control, these psychological symptoms lessen or disappear. If there were deep-seated psychological problems, this would not be the case. The fact that there is no single psychological cause for compulsive overeating and bulimia, and that despite years of research experts still cannot find a definitive cause for these disorders, suggests that they do not originate with our state of mind but the state of our bodies. Psychologists, psychiatrists and experts in eating disorders have come up with varying convoluted and complex hypotheses for the psychological causes for compulsive eating and bulimia, including personality disorders and psychosis, but have failed to look at the simplest physical basis for overeating. There will, of course, be a percentage of compulsive overeaters and bulimics who do have deep-seated psychological problems, as there is in any cross-section of society. There may be cases where childhood abuse or other negative childhood experiences have contributed to or caused eating disorders. These people need the help of psychology and counselling, and it is important that if you feel there is a lot more to your problem than a physiological imbalance, as suggested in this book, you seek the help you need. Here we are addressing the majority of psychologically normal people who are simply reacting to the lack of control over their compulsive eating or bulimia.

As we have seen, compulsive overeating and food addiction are caused by eating foods that we have become intolerant or addicted to because we are not genetically built to cope with them. We are effectively putting poisons into our body in the same way that alcoholics, smokers and drug addicts do. We eat compulsively because we have become addicted to certain foods, and we purge and vomit after overeating in order to regain some control over the addiction and prevent weight gain.

Perhaps the type of food we are obliged to eat during childhood sets us up for food intolerances and addictions during adolescence or in later life. If we overeat certain food groups such as grains or refined sugar throughout our early years, and continue to eat them in adulthood, we can overload our bodies with substances we are not designed to cope with.

The solution

Is there any hope for us after all this? Of course there is, and the solutions are relatively easy. There are just a few golden rules to follow if you want to be free from cravings, compulsive eating and bulimia, be naturally slim without dieting and regain the optimum health and vitality that is a normal and natural part of the human physiology that has evolved over millions of years.

- Eat fresh, natural, nutrient-dense food (real food!). Around 65 per cent of our ancestors' diets consisted of fresh vegetables, fruit, nuts and seeds, which are full of nutrients, and the remaining 35 per cent came from wild meats such as game and seafood, which are low in saturated fat and high in omega-3 fatty acids. We will develop a strategy for this later that will fit in with your lifestyle and your own food preferences, but to adhere strictly to a diet similar to the one our ancestors ate, you should eat lean meat, fish and seafood as well as plenty of non-starchy vegetables (dark green leafy vegetables rather than potatoes), and cut out cereals, dairy products and all processed foods (including bread, cakes, convenience foods, sweets, many canned foods, pastas). No calorie counting necessary!
- Develop the 80:20 rule (or 90:10 if you are trying to lose weight). The majority of your food should be fresh, natural foods, but you can allow yourself a few modern foods and treats. This way,

you can eat healthily and still plan in a little indulgence. Even our ancestors enjoyed a little honey when they could get it. Just make sure your treats are not your trigger foods.

- Stay active and mentally alert. Our ancestors walked miles and were fit and lean. They had to stay mentally alert in order to survive. You too need to be physically and mentally active, and we will devise ways you can do this in your personalized plan.

- Learn to cope with anger, negative emotions and stress. Modern life presents many insidious pressures and stresses our ancestors didn't have. They also had more balance in their lives, with days of activity and hunting interspersed with times of relaxation and socializing. You need to de-stress too and learn to deal with anger and negative emotions quickly and effectively so that you don't end up de-stressing with food.

- Have a purpose in life. Too often we spend our time in pointless activities and end up bored, dissatisfied and unfulfilled. No wonder we turn to food for comfort. When your life has meaning and you feel happy and satisfied that you are striving to reach your full potential, your focus changes.

8

Finding your personal lifetime plan

Now that you have an explanation for why you have developed compulsive eating or bulimia, you are in a position to overcome it, shed any excess weight you may have, and live a normal life once again. This is an exciting prospect and it is so easy to achieve once you are free of the cravings that characterize food intolerances, food addictions, compulsive eating and bulimia. This chapter will help you prepare a plan that will keep you healthy, slim and free of compulsive eating and bulimia for life. In order to achieve this we need to:

1 prepare to change;
2 take control by cutting out all substances that cause food cravings;
3 think straight, free of food cravings and plan how you will manage your lifetime diet;
4 substitute natural, healthy foods for unhealthy ones;
5 choose your treats carefully and plan how you will incorporate them into your diet using the 80:20 rule;
6 treat your problems with food as seriously as any alcoholic, smoker or drug addict should if they are to overcome their problems with addictive substances;
7 use exercise as a road to physical and emotional health;
8 love yourself better and address emotional issues that contribute to the problem;
9 find purpose in your life.

Preparing for change

Change can be exciting but it can also bring anxieties. You have probably lived with compulsive overeating or bulimia for years and the prospect of being free of the condition is wonderful and scary at the same time. Despite desperately wanting to change your eating habits, compulsive eating has been part of your life for a long time. You want this change to be permanent and you want to give it your best shot, so I suggest a few days of preparation before you take control and rid yourself of the compulsive need to eat – for ever. This is period of reprogramming your brain and your subconscious to accept the changes you are about to make. It's about making a special decision to be proactive and take control of your eating and your life. Only you can do it.

For the next few days, keep a food diary and record everything you eat and at what times of the day, so you can understand your current patterns and find ways to substitute unhealthy habits for healthy ones. Try to identify possible trigger foods that you may be intolerant or addicted to and think about how you will incorporate the changes you will read about in this book into your life. Think about your social and family life and how the changes you make will affect you and the people you care about, and look forward to becoming free of food cravings and addictions. Feel happy at the prospect of being free, plan your new wardrobe for when you are slim, and visualize yourself as the new person you want to be – slim, happy and free of compulsive eating and bulimia. When you have read the next chapter on how to love yourself better, think about how you can incorporate these ideas into your life to give yourself the best chance of success.

You can make practical preparations, such as sorting out your fridge, freezer and food cupboards. If you live alone, this should be relatively easy, but if you share your home with others, think about how you can get their support so that you can make changes to your diet. Get rid of tins and packets of food you know will be a problem to you, and make space in the fridge for lots of fresh natural food. If others in the household have a stash of sugary foods, don't taunt yourself with them, but ask that they be kept away from the main food cupboards and out of temptation. It might even be worth keeping your food in a separate cupboard and a separate part of the fridge if the rest of the household won't join you in a healthier eating plan – it could benefit everyone. Why torture yourself? Write a shopping list for the foods you will buy in preparation to take control. When you have read the next chapter, you will be in a position to plan your meals. Use these few days to do that and buy in the correct foods.

Start taking more exercise, walk more, and start to build muscle in your body for fat burning and keeping your metabolic rate high. Exercise produces endorphins and 'feel good' chemicals in your brain, so walk to feel good and de-stress. Walking gives you time to yourself to think and plan and visualize your new life free of compulsions to eat. This sort of time is important and will contribute to your success. We will look at exercise again later, but in these few days of preparation you should begin to get into the habit of walking or taking more of your favourite exercise. Start drinking more pure water. Get yourself a very large glass and keep it next to the sink. Have a drink of water every time you're in the kitchen to rehydrate yourself and get into the habit of drinking pure water. It will help to make you feel fuller and help to clear out toxins from your body. We generally don't drink enough pure water, so drink up – it's good for you. Try to get plenty of rest and sleep too. When we are tired and crabby it's hard to make big changes. Try to get a few early nights and some time for relaxation in these few days of preparation.

Plan when you will start, and commit yourself to a date within the next week or so. Check what social engagements you have ahead. You need to set aside at least a week or ten days where you do not have social events at which you will be expected to eat, such as at parties, restaurants or get-togethers. This is important. Give yourself a fair chance and make things easy on yourself. If you can't find a whole week to get in control, then you have to make one – it's as simple as that. If you came down with the flu, you'd be forced to have a week off to get better. Treat this as seriously as any illness, and find time to devote to sorting yourself out. Think of it as preparing to go into rehab, as any drug addict would. The problem really is that serious, and your addictions are as strong as any other addict's, so be prepared. If you want to, even have a final binge as a symbolic farewell to all the foods you'll be living without for a while, then on your appointed day – take control.

9

Take control of your food

As we have seen, compulsive overeating and bulimia can be caused by food intolerances, food sensitivities and food addictions. The only way to treat these conditions or free yourself from any addiction is to stop taking these substances into your body. With tobacco, alcohol and drugs, it is relatively straightforward because you know which substances you are addicted to. You have to give them up and stay away from them afterwards. The problem with food addiction is that we still have to eat, and the trick is knowing which foods are causing the problem. You could take a food intolerance test to identify the problem foods. However, by doing this you are only tackling part of the problem. A test may show that you are intolerant to a certain food, such as wheat, and you could cut out all foods from your diet that contain wheat, such as bread, pasta, cereals and crackers. This would certainly help, but there is still the problem with refined sugar and fats that has not been addressed with this approach. These foods contribute to hypoglycaemia and diseases such as heart disease, hypertension and diabetes. You may find that although you have cut out one food group that is causing problems, it has not cured your compulsive eating or bulimia because you are still eating refined sugar, which also causes food cravings. You may be simply transferring your compulsion to overeat to other foods, which may even make the problem worse. In order to tackle compulsive eating and bulimia, you have to take a radical approach to your diet as a whole.

From what you have read so far, you know which foods are the likely candidates for food intolerance and food addiction, and they are the ones that our bodies are not genetically adapted to deal with. They are the grains and cereals, such as wheat, barley, maize and oats; milk and dairy products; refined sugar in any form; and modified or hydrogenated fats, such as margarine, and shortening in baked goods. These are the foods you are most likely to crave and overeat.

When you stop eating foods you have become addicted to, you will experience withdrawal symptoms and intense cravings as you would with any other addiction. There is no other way to beat it than to cut out these offending foods and substances.

There are two ways you can take control and cut them out of your diet:

1 Take a radical approach and stop eating them immediately ('cold turkey').
2 Cut out the offending foods gradually over three to four weeks.

The approach you take largely depends on your personality and the way you wish to deal with the problem. There are pros and cons with both methods. If you take a radical approach and cut out these foods immediately, you are likely to experience intense cravings for a few days while they clear from your body completely. This should take no longer than four to five days. This means that after four to five days you are back in control and on the way to beating compulsive eating and bulimia for ever. You will have experienced a few days of very unpleasant symptoms as if you were unwell, but if you think you could cope with this then it is probably the quickest and most effective way to get control. A few days should not affect the rest of your life too much, and you will not be subjecting your-self to too many food temptations when socializing or shopping. Although you will need will-power and determination for a few days, you will be containing the problem and getting it over with quickly.

If you decide to take the longer route and cut out these foods over three to four weeks, you will still experience withdrawal symptoms and cravings but they should be less intense. If you are determined and can stick to a longer period of withdrawal, then you might find this method better, but it does prolong the agony. There is also the risk that over several weeks you will be subjecting yourself to the temptation of food when shopping or socializing. You have to have iron will-power and the determina-tion to succeed over a prolonged period. I would advise the radical approach every time as it will give you control quickly and reduce the period of withdrawal to a few days. You should feel better and more able to move on to plan your eating while you have a mind to succeed with it. The danger with a prolonged period of withdrawing problem foods is that you may fall back into your old familiar habits and end up back at square one. Once the offending food has cleared from your system in just a few days, you should have no further problems and the cravings will disappear. You will feel so much better, in control, and free of the long list of physiological and psychological symptoms we saw earlier. Here is a reminder of these symptoms: an insatiable craving for particular foods, bloating, constipation, diarrhoea, irritable bowel syndrome, indigestion and heartburn, flatulence, weight fluctuations and weight gain, water retention, headaches, fatigue and listlessness, exhaustion, dizziness, hot flushes, trembling and faintness when hungry, feeling cold after eating, insomnia, aching muscles, cramp, coated tongue, constant thirst, breathing problems such as gasping for air, constant yawning or chest tightness, anxiety, depression, moodiness and irritability.

When you cut out problem foods from your diet, you will eliminate all these symptoms and feel better than you have in years. You will finally be able to take control of your eating and make logical and reasoned decisions about what you eat, rather than be driven to eat unhealthy foods that your body craves because of addiction. You will also lose weight rapidly and find your clothes will fit better. You will begin to feel successful and full of hope for the future.

What can you eat freely in order to gain control?

- Fresh lean meat (beef, lamb, pork, bacon, ham, chicken, turkey, rabbit, duck and game)
- Fresh fish (plaice, haddock, cod, turbot, halibut, mackerel, salmon, tuna, pilchard, shellfish) and tinned fish with no added ingredients
- Tofu or Quorn
- Salad
- Fresh vegetables, including root vegetables (but see below for potatoes)
- You can cook in olive oil and you can use butter
- You can have natural yoghurt (preferably live)
- Eggs – chicken or duck eggs

- Fresh herbs and spices
- You can drink water, black tea and coffee
- Food can be grilled, boiled, steamed, baked, roasted with olive oil, microwaved or stir-fried with olive oil. Do not fry foods and try to remove fat from meat before cooking.

What foods must you limit in order to gain control?

You can eat the following foods, but in limited quantities and no more than once a day:

- A small baked potato (up to 200 g/7 oz)
- 80 g/3 oz of wholegrain or wild rice (weighed dry before cooking)
- One medium banana
- One apple or pear
- One orange or grapefruit
- One cupful of berries or grapes
- A few nuts or seeds (less than a handful)
- Two level tablespoons of mayonnaise

What must you stop eating altogether in order to gain control?

- No processed or refined sugar – no cakes, biscuits, sweets, chocolate or processed sugary foods
- No fruit other than listed above
- No processed meat such as corned beef or tinned meat with preservatives, etc.
- No processed fish such as fishcakes
- No grains (other than 80 g/3 oz of wholegrain or wild rice). So no wheat, bran, barley, oats or maize. No bread, crackers, breakfast cereals, cereal bars, pasta or wheat snacks
- No white or flavoured rice or noodles
- No canned foods such as baked beans, macaroni cheese or spaghetti or packet sauces and flavourings
- No milk, cream, cheese or ice cream
- No crisps, salted nuts or salty snacks
- No mushrooms (to eliminate candida)
- No alcohol
- No fruit juices, sugary soft drinks and no sugary hot chocolate drinks

Ideas for meals

When you limit your usual variety of foods you may be stumped as to what you can put together for meals, so here are a few suggestions to choose from.

Breakfasts

Kedgeree (wholegrain or wild rice with fish)
Allowed fruit and natural yoghurt with a few nuts or seeds
Haddock and eggs
Salad
Leftover vegetables with a knob of butter
Bacon and eggs
Scrambled eggs with ham
Omelette

Lunches

Salad and a baked potato
Kedgeree
Meat or fish with salad or vegetables
Allowed fruit
Stir-fried vegetables with meat or fish
Homemade soup using allowed ingredients

Snacks

Nuts or seeds
Allowed fruit
Leftover vegetables warmed in a microwave with a knob of butter or mayonnaise
A raw carrot
A couple of sticks of celery and some nuts
A pot of natural live yoghurt

Evening meals

Meat and salad or vegetables
Fish and salad or vegetables
Kedgeree with salad or vegetables
Stir-fried vegetables with meat or fish

Homemade curry with wholegrain or wild rice
A baked potato, meat or fish with salad or vegetables

Fruit is limited for four to five days because of the high sugar content in fruit. Although this is natural sugar and you are encouraged to eat fruit when you are back in control, it is important to get your insulin mechanism and hypoglycaemia under control. If you have developed insulin resistance, it is necessary to give your body a rest from sugar so that you regain a proper balance of glucose in your body. If you can, stick to one banana a day, but do have *some* fruit if you are struggling.

Try cooking extra vegetables and put them in bowls to warm up in a microwave as snacks and use leftovers of kedgeree for an evening treat. Save nuts and seeds to nibble in the evenings and have a few hard-boiled eggs prepared in the fridge to quell hunger pangs between meals.

Try some bacon bits as a snack or salad/stir-fry garnish. Chop up some lean bacon slices into bits and microwave for a few minutes. Try chopped hard-boiled eggs mixed with a little mayonnaise as a filler for a baked potato to eat with a salad.

Instead of a glass of wine, try a still or sparkling mineral water.

You shouldn't restrict the amounts of food that you are allowed to eat. You may be experiencing intense cravings and withdrawal symptoms, so be nice to yourself and eat plenty of the foods you *can* eat. You should lose weight quite dramatically but don't worry about this at the moment, especially if insulin resistance may have been a problem. Eat as much food as you need to to satisfy your hunger; you can adjust your diet in the next stage if you want to slim down. The crucial thing is that you get your eating under control and eliminate cravings. Until you do this, you are a prisoner of your compulsive eating and bulimia.

Continue this eating regime for at least four to five days, preferably a week. It should only take about four to five days for the foods that have been causing you problems to clear from your system but, if you can, keep at it for a few more days just to make sure. You may feel quite unwell at times, with intense cravings, headaches, dizziness and general lethargy. This is just your body experiencing withdrawal symptoms from foods to which you are intolerant, and the worse you feel, the more of a problem you may have had with these foods – so it is all the more important to get under control. If you go back to eating the wrong foods, you simply prolong the agony and remain a prisoner of your compulsive eating and bulimia. Please stay with it and hang in there for a few days. Take to your bed with a magazine if you have to, but whatever you do, do not eat the foods that are causing you problems. Once you get over these few days, you will feel in control of your eating, you will have a clear head and feel well; in fact probably better than you have for years. It is all so worthwhile, so hang in there.

If you are eliminating problem foods gradually, then over a period of three weeks, eliminate each food group on the 'not allowed' list one by one until you are on the complete radical plan, then stay on this for four to five days. You will need discipline to stick at it, particularly when you experience cravings as you eliminate food groups, but it can be done. The main thing is to get quickly to the point where you are only eating the foods on the 'allowed list' and stay there for four to five days to clear all the problem foods from your body.

A summary of how you may feel

- During the first few days you may experience intense cravings, headache, dizziness, lethargy and you may feel quite unwell. If this happens, it just means your body is getting rid of the toxic substances that have accumulated due to an unsuitable diet. The worse you feel, the more of a problem you may have. Rest and drink plenty of pure water and eat lots of the foods on the 'allowed' list.
- After a few days you will probably feel much better. The cravings should disappear, and you should feel in control of your eating, with headaches and dizziness diminishing, and more energy than you may have had in years. As your blood glucose stabilizes, you will feel less shaky and irritable. You will be able to think with a clearer head – no more fuzzy thinking. Any gastrointestinal symptoms, such as heartburn, indigestion, bloating and irritable bowel syndrome, will start to improve. In short, you will start to eliminate symptoms on the long list we saw earlier, and should feel better than you have in a long time. Now you are in a position logically to plan your lifetime eating habits.

- After a few months of eating fresh natural foods, your body becomes well nourished and your physiological and metabolic mechanisms work in balance and harmony as they are meant to. You may notice that you do not crave foods any more and that you are satisfied with less food. This is because your body is getting all the nutrients it needs and the hunger mechanisms we met earlier in the book are working to get you to eat the right amount of food for your body. It doesn't need huge amounts of nutritionally poor processed foods in order to get the right ingredients for maintaining your body in peak condition. Your tastes may change and processed food may become distasteful; for example you will probably find that sugar is too sweet and that you dislike the cloying chemical taste of many modern foods. This is when you know you will never want to go back to your old eating habits again.

Beat your immediate food triggers

When we have been emotionally and physically habituated to faulty eating, sometimes for many years, it is easy to eat without really thinking about it. Eating becomes part of your subconscious conditioning and it may take some conscious effort to adopt a different pattern of eating and to eat foods different from those you normally would. It may feel very strange to be eating foods you are not accustomed to eating, and the temptation will be to give in to cravings and make a vow to 'start again tomorrow'. This is the worst thing you could possibly do. You will only prolong the agony – you have to do it some time, so you may as well get it over with and do it now. Another reason is that by putting it off again and again, you are sending the message to yourself and your subconscious that it is not important enough to make an effort and that your immediate need for a particular food is more important than overcoming your eating problems. You simply perpetuate and exacerbate the problem physically and psychologically. This is a sure way to stay stuck with your problems for ever.

The first few days of getting your eating under control are crucial, and this is when you will need the most help and support. You may be used to turning to food when you are upset, or perhaps you automatically give yourself permission to eat anything during family get-togethers or at other social events. This is why you should protect this vital period of time and give yourself every chance of succeeding so that you can break free of food addictions for good. Don't plan a drastic alteration to your diet when you have social events in your diary, and make sure you don't have temptation foods in your cupboards. Give yourself a proper chance. You will almost certainly experience intense cravings during the first few days as you take control of your eating. These can be distressing but, as with any addiction, they are a necessary step to breaking free. You now realize how important it is to regain control and eradicate these addictive substances from your diet if you are to overcome compulsive eating and bulimia. I can't stress how important it is that you refrain from eating problem foods.

What about those absent moments when you reach for some item of food or it dawns on you that you have wandered out to the kitchen and have your head in the fridge searching for food for the umpteenth time? What happens when you are struck with the munchies when you are watching TV or you just had a row with your boss at work? You just *have* to have something to chew on?

Try these suggestions:

- A handy substitute such as sugar-free chewing gum. The minty taste will help curb your desire for the food item you were after, and it gives you something to chew.
- Brush your teeth. Again, the minty taste is a deterrent.
- Go out for a walk to distract you from food. Exercise can also act as a natural appetite suppressant.
- Write out on a card all the reasons why you want to do this and why you want it to work. On one side of the card have all the positive aspects of getting on top of compulsive eating, such as relief from those ghastly symptoms we talked about before, the freedom from being controlled by food and how lovely you will look when you have the figure you want. Also put on the card that the cravings will only last a few days – then you will be free. On the other side of the card, list all the consequences of not sticking to your eating plan: the fact that food will continue to control your life and make you depressed and unhappy, and the persistence of feeling ill and lethargic. Make several copies and have them laminated. Keep them

handy around the house and in your handbag and fix them to the fridge and to the food cupboards. When you feel an overwhelming craving, stop and read your card to remind yourself how vital it is that you regain your resolve to gain control of your eating.

- Plan an absorbing project that will take up all your time during the first few days. How about an intricate knitting pattern to get stuck into that keeps your hands busy or a painting by numbers kit, a course of study, a challenging project at work or even preparing a vegetable plot in the garden for all those glorious fresh vegetables you could grow for yourself? The main thing is to take your mind off food and be too busy to dwell on it.

- Play an audio tape that you have recorded for yourself giving all the reasons why you must stick to your plan.

- Take a deep breath, close your eyes and relax. Meditate on your inner strength and imagine you are totally in control and beating this demon once and for all. Develop a powerful visualization that you are conquering your eating problem. Make it dramatic, such as a picture of you bashing all your forbidden foods with a stick, then sweeping the tattered remains away and out of your life. Feel strong and forceful about it, determined never to let food control you again.

Thinking straight and planning

Once you are back in control of your eating, and free of the awful cravings associated with food intolerance and food addiction, you will feel better and more able to think clearly and develop a lifelong eating plan that will help keep you in control and free of compulsive eating and bulimia.

In order to take control, you had to be strict about the foods you ate in order to stop the cravings associated with food intolerance and addiction, but a lifelong eating plan has to be sustainable and fit in with our modern lives. It has to ensure that you are able to maintain control over your eating and it must eliminate compulsive food cravings. It has to be individual and tailored to suit you.

Now that you are in control, have a look at the food list you wrote at the beginning. How do you feel about these foods now? Do you feel deprived because you know that the foods you have been craving are the very foods that you must limit or eliminate from your diet? Or do you feel liberated knowing that you are now free of the foods that kept you imprisoned in compulsive overeating and bulimia? Perhaps you feel a mixture of both. Try to identify foods on your list that have been causing problems and eliminate them from your life. Is all the misery worth continuing to eat what is effectively a poison? There are so many wonderful, health-giving foods available, you will never feel deprived.

What can you eat on the lifetime plan?

- Fresh lean meat (beef, lamb, pork, bacon, ham, chicken, turkey, rabbit, duck and game)
- Fresh fish (plaice, haddock, cod, turbot, halibut, mackerel, salmon, tuna, pilchard, shellfish) and tinned fish with no added ingredients
- Tofu or Quorn
- Salad
- Fresh vegetables including root vegetables (go easy with potatoes)
- Fresh whole fruit
- Wholegrain or wild rice (occasional white rice)
- Nuts and seeds
- You can cook in olive oil and you can use butter
- You can have natural yoghurt (preferably live)
- Mayonnaise (but go easy)
- Eggs – chicken or duck eggs
- Fresh herbs and spices

You can drink water, a little milk in tea and coffee and low-calorie or sugar-free drinks in moderation.

Food can be grilled, boiled, steamed, baked, roasted with olive oil, microwaved or stir-fried with olive oil. Do not fry foods and try to remove fat from meat before cooking.

What must you generally eliminate from your diet?

- No processed or refined sugar – no cakes, biscuits, sweets, chocolate or processed sugary foods
- No processed meat such as corned beef or tinned meat with preservatives, etc.
- No processed fish such as fishcakes

- No grains – wheat, bran, barley, oats or maize. No bread, crackers, breakfast cereals, cereal bars, pasta or wheat snacks
- No canned foods such as baked beans, macaroni cheese or spaghetti or packet sauces and flavourings
- No crisps, salted nuts or salty snacks
- No fruit juices or sugary soft drinks. Low-calorie and sugar-free drinks should be all right in moderation.

(There are recipe suggestions towards the end of the book.)

You will still have to stay away from potentially problem foods such as grains and refined sugar, but after four to six weeks, if you want to reintroduce these foods you can carefully introduce one food at a time and monitor your reaction to it. It may be possible to start eating a food that you have been intolerant to once again, but you must reintroduce it carefully and in a limited way if you are to avoid becoming addicted again. My advice is that if you have identified a trigger food that you know will set you off bingeing, then avoid it like the plague. Just as an ex-smoker has to avoid tobacco, or a heroin addict has to stay away from heroin, you will have to accept that a particular food is addictive for you and stay away from it. It is better to be healthy and in control than to taste a food that will end up causing you heartache and misery. You will be surprised at how quickly you will become used to not eating bread, crackers and cereals, or sugary processed foods. Your friends and family will become used to it and it will no longer be of any concern to anyone. We all have dietary preferences and these will become yours.

You will probably find that after following a diet rich in fresh, natural foods for even just a few days, your tastes will change and just as an ex-smoker comes to hate the smell of tobacco smoke, you will come to dislike the taste of sugary or starchy processed food. There is nothing like the clean feeling you get on the inside when you eat nature's food rather than the cloying chemical taste and the coated tongue you get when you eat processed food.

If you want to follow a diet that your body is genetically adapted to cope with, my advice is to steer clear of all processed food and stick to nature's food as far as possible. Adopt the 80:20 rule and you won't go far wrong.

Develop the 80:20 rule

The 80:20 rule (or the 90:10 if you want to lose weight) is to ensure that for the majority of the time (80 or 90 per cent of the time) you eat fresh natural foods, nature's food, but you also have some leeway for modern convenience when you need it. It may be difficult to make sure you always eat the right food when you're in a hurry, and it's nice to have a little indulgence now and again. A little of what you fancy might well do you good, but you can also have too much of a good thing. Always remember that eating a particular food could trigger your compulsive eating or bulimia again. Is it worth that?

Generally, eat fresh, natural, nutrient-dense food. You should eat lean meat, fish and seafood as well as plenty of non-starchy vegetables (dark green leafy vegetables rather than too many potatoes); cut out cereals, dairy products and all processed foods, including bread, cakes, convenience foods, sweets, many canned foods, pastas. You will quickly adjust to this, particularly when you remember that to go back may trigger your compulsive eating or bulimia again. Think of this diet plan as your medicine that will keep you well and in control of your eating. It will also eliminate all those symptoms you may have suffered such as bloating and digestive problems, depression and lethargy.

Changing your dietary habits may mean monitoring every mouthful at first until healthy eating becomes your new habit. Every time you go to put something in your mouth, think about the effects it will have on your health and weight. Is this a trigger food that will set me off on a cycle of compulsive overeating? Is it worth sacrificing my health and the progress I'm making to eat this food now? Would I rather be in control of my eating than have this food now, which is just a temporary fix?

Treat your compulsive overeating as seriously as giving up smoking, alcohol or drugs. You have been suffering from a catalogue of food addictions and the only way to stop the awful cravings is to stop taking the addictive substance into your body. You have identified which substances are likely to be addictive, and so you must stop putting them into your body. The alternative is to let food continue to control your life.

Stop dieting and lose weight

Remember that the feeling of fullness and the satiation of hunger is brought about by the weight of food in your stomach as well as the chemical content of the food. Therefore, a pound of nutrient-dense vegetables will satisfy your hunger as well as a pound of fried chips and hamburgers, and because the constituents in the vegetables satisfy the nutritional needs of your body, you will not end up craving more and more calorie-rich food in order to get the right nutrients.

When you stop eating processed food and eat natural whole foods like fruit, vegetables and lean meat, you automatically cut down on salt, sugar, fat and calories. It becomes easy to maintain a healthy body, feel well and full of energy and to attain the correct weight.

If you find you are still not losing the weight you want, try cutting down on foods that have a higher carbohydrate content. You can eliminate or substitute a few items at a time until you start to lose weight. The trick is to reduce carbohydrates that have a higher proportion of starch or sugar. We have learned that refined carbohydrates contain huge amounts of unhealthy carbohydrates, but even fruit and vegetables consist of carbohydrates and some have a higher natural carbohydrate content than others. In order to lose weight you can substitute for these foods with a lower carbohydrate content.

For the following high-carbohydrate foods you could substitute those on the second, low-carbohydrate foods list to help you kick-start your weight loss without radically altering your new dietary plan. Starchy and sugary processed foods such as bread, pasta and processed meats have been left out since they are not part of your diet. They are nearly all high-carbohydrate foods and should be avoided. Your aim is still to eat fresh, natural foods. Cut out dressings and sauces, which often contain sugar. You will be surprised how quickly you will become accustomed to eating food without these. Try a knob of butter on runner beans or a baked potato instead.

Eat plenty of protein, meat, fish or vegetarian proteins such as tofu as this will help to satisfy your appetite. And remember when you are trying to lose weight that the more slowly you lose it, the more chance you have of keeping it off permanently, so don't be in too much of a rush. The secret is to make changes you can live with on a permanent basis. By making the above substitutions, you should be able to include foods on the high-carbohydrate list again when you have reached your ideal weight because they are also natural healthy foods. You should be able to maintain your desired weight since you will never be returning to a 'normal' diet full of refined and processed food that will disrupt your blood glucose and cause food intolerances, food addictions and overeating. Also, make sure you are not exceeding ten per cent of your food intake in treats, as it is easy to judge this incorrectly. Treats should be the first thing to cut down on if you wish to lose weight.

Aim to lose one to two pounds per week and you have a much better chance of sticking to your diet and keeping the weight off permanently. If later on you do put on a couple of pounds again, just go back to this strategy of substitution for a few weeks. Remember that a slow steady weight loss is infinitely better than the vicious cycle of bingeing and starving with its inevitable upward spiral of weight increase. If you lost just one pound per week you would lose half a stone every seven weeks and three and a half in a year! What would you weigh a year from now if you didn't adopt this eating plan?

Managing your weight and the correct diet is for life. As we have seen, 'slimming diets' don't work and so you have to accept that your normal diet is something you have to manage on a continuous basis. Our eating habits are largely a result of the habits we have adopted over many years. Habits are learned and can just as

High-carbohydrate foods

Broad beans	Kiwi fruit
Haricot beans	Nectarine
Lentils	Orange
Red kidney beans	Peach
Salad dressings	Pear
Soya beans	Tinned fruit
Sweet potatoes	Cantaloupe
Calf liver	Honeydew melon
Apple	Watermelon
Apricot	Raisins
Avocado	Honey
Banana	Beer
Fruit juices	

Medium- and low-carbohydrate foods

Beef

Lamb

Pork

Chicken

Turkey

Fish – all types of
fresh or tinned
fish

Cheese

Eggs

Butter

Olive oil

Mayonnaise

Nuts and seeds
(in moderation)

Blackberries

Blueberries

Cherries

Cranberries

Grapes
(in moderation)

Mango

Melon

Papaya

Pineapple

Plum

Raspberries

Rhubarb

Strawberries

Watermelon

Asparagus

Aubergine

French and
runner
beans

Broccoli

Brussels sprouts

Cabbage

Carrot

Cauliflower

Celery

Cucumber

Endive

Fennel

Mixed green leaves

Kale

Leek

Lettuce

Mushrooms

Okra

Onion

Peas, garden

Peppers (all colours)

White potatoes (in
moderation)

Pumpkin

Spinach

Sweetcorn (in moderation)

Tomatoes, fresh or tinned

Turnip

Watercress

Tofu

Soya milk

Wine

Rum

Vodka

easily be unlearned and replaced with new healthy habits. That is the remarkable thing about human beings; we are adaptable, flexible and very fast learners. Our brain has an infinite capacity to change and support our desired behaviours and we can draw upon this flexibility to change our thinking and our habits around food.

Medical support

If you have any medical concerns at all or you are very obese, you should see your family doctor. He or she may suggest a course of counselling, psychotherapy or cognitive behavioural therapy (CBT) that will help you address any psychological problems you may be having, and may help you develop a healthier attitude to your diet.

Your doctor may also prescribe antidepressant drugs, which has been a traditional form of first-line treatment. There are limitations, however, with antidepressants, and although people taking these drugs tend to binge less often, they do not stop bingeing altogether and so the root cause of the problem remains. Antidepressants do not have any effect on a person's diet and nutritional needs or on the starve–binge cycle of dieting. Also, the effects of antidepressants do not last. People tend to relapse after a period of taking the drugs. The main problem with taking drugs of any sort is that you are not addressing the cause of the problem – and *that* is the unsuitable diet you have been subjecting your body to. You also have to suffer the effects of coming off the drugs eventually. The medical profession, as well as psychologists and counsellors, tend to approach problems with eating as psychological disorders without considering the physical causes in our diet.

Your doctor can prescribe antidepressants, suggest further psychological help, advise on a healthy diet and provide support and encouragement, but ultimately you have to take steps to help yourself. No one can do it for you.

Functional foods and supplements

Functional foods is a term used by the nutrition and chemical industry to describe foods with added nutritional value, mainly foods such as dairy foods and cereals. They frequently make claims of increased health or medical benefits and are becoming increasingly complex and technologically diverse. There is a huge growth in probiotics and prebiotics, usually added to yoghurts and desserts, which modify gut flora and increase the growth of beneficial gut bacteria. Another growing section of the functional foods market is in antioxidants and, more recently, flavonoids, which are claimed to protect us from cancers, heart disease and other conditions. Antioxidants are being extracted from fruits and vegetables and supplies of another health-giving ingredient, omega-3 fatty acids (found in oily fish such as salmon), are being genetically engineered in plants to provide supplements for functional foods.

Large sugar-refining companies are investing huge amounts of venture capital to fund the development of these functional foods as consumer demand increases. The general market for functional foods is worth over $36 billion across the USA, Japan and the EU, and yet there is limited scientific evidence that they actually have the beneficial effects being claimed by the industry. Around 60–70 per cent of applications for approval of these products are being turned down by the EU regulatory body and the Food and Drug Administration (FDA) in the USA because there is insufficient evidence to support their claims.

For example, over 223 published scientific studies on the antioxidant effects of green tea concluded that the drink is 'highly unlikely' to reduce the risks of cancer, and yet manufacturers continue to make such claims. The probiotics added to yoghurts in the UK have been found to contain inadequate levels of bacteria to be effective, and yet the products continue to sell.

We know so little about the combined effects of ingredients being added to food that we are tampering with nature's rich harvest to produce so-called food that has at best dubious health benefits. Rather than get our omega-3s from genetically engineered supplements, why not get them naturally from fish in our diet? And instead of taking supplements to supply antioxidants, why not eat the whole fruits they are extracted from, the way nature intended? Natural food has the right ingredients in the right proportions for our bodies. And why eat cereal and bread that is so nutritionally poor it has to be fortified with chemicals? If you feel you need a nutritional supplement, which shouldn't really be necessary when you eat a naturally healthy diet, why not opt for a good all-round A–Z vitamin and mineral supplement? You shouldn't really need anything else – after all, our ancestors managed perfectly well without them.

Summary of the main points

- Take control by cutting out all substances that cause food cravings, food intolerances and addictions.
- Once you are back in control, plan how you will manage your lifetime diet.
- Choose your treats carefully and plan how you will incorporate them into your diet. Adopt the 80:20 rule (or the 90:10 rule if you want to lose weight).
- Stop dieting and lose weight naturally and permanently.
- Treat your problems with food as seriously as any alcoholic, smoker or drug addict should if they are to overcome their problems with addictive substances.

10

Exercise for physical and emotional health

Our ancestors walked miles, exercised vigorously in their daily life and were fit and lean. They had to stay mentally alert in order to survive and they were forced to do hard work in order to get the next meal. They too, if given the choice, would probably have preferred to have been relaxing around the campfire and, indeed, they had a cycle of days of intense activity and exercise interspersed with days of relaxation. Modern humans live incredibly sedentary lives in comparison. Technology has allowed us to do less physical work and we don't need to go on long arduous foraging or hunting trips; we simply drive the car to the supermarket. Yet we need to be physically and mentally active if we are to be healthy. Our bodies start to break down when we become sedentary with stiffness, lethargy and obesity. Regular vigorous exercise is normal for humans – it is abnormal to be sedentary.

The benefits of exercise

The following list shows some of the amazing benefits of exercise:

- maintains weight loss over the long term;
- increases resting metabolic rate;
- improves strength and stamina;
- improves muscle tone;
- improves joint flexibility and suppleness;
- strengthens back muscles and eases back pain;
- strengthens heart muscle;
- improves lung function;
- improves digestion;
- helps reduce food cravings and regulates appetite;

- slows down the body's ageing process and helps you look better;
- reduces stress and anxiety;
- improves your mental clarity;
- elevates mood;
- increases self-esteem and self-confidence;
- increases energy and reduces fatigue;
- increases the production of endorphins helping you feel calm;
- helps you sleep better;
- reduces the risk of heart disease;
- lowers blood pressure;
- reduces the risk of osteoporosis and increases bone density;
- reduces the risk of mature onset diabetes;
- improves your insulin/blood glucose mechanism;
- restores cholesterol to healthy levels;
- it feels good!

Just a long walk three times a week will help improve your level of fitness and increase your mental and physical well-being. A programme of exercise that incorporates stretching, cardiovascular or aerobic work and strength/resistance training is even better and will result in an all-over level of fitness. If you have been sedentary for a long time, are very unfit or overweight, do see your GP for a check-up before embarking on unaccustomed exercise. Start gently and keep pushing yourself to work harder so that your body improves its level of fitness. Remember to wear loose-fitting, comfortable clothes for exercise and properly fitting shoes.

Make exercise interesting as well as more effective by varying your activities. Try walking a few days a week then swimming or cycling. Incorporate some strength-training exercises and stretching, and don't forget to warm up before exercise and cool down after and drink extra water when you exercise to correct dehydration. If you need some guidance on the right exercise programme for you, join a gym or go to your local fitness centre. Try to make exercise fun. Why not have fun too – put on some music and have a dance around the room, or get a skipping rope and get skipping! You could get pedalling on an exercise bike while you watch TV. Also increase your lifestyle activity by walking more instead of driving, using the stairs rather than the lift and generally moving more. It's all good exercise!

As a weight-loss strategy on its own, exercise is not very effective. To burn up a pound of fat, you need to use 3,500 calories, which amounts to a lot of exercise. It is eating the correct diet that will result in weight loss, but exercise will help you keep the weight off long term. Exercise improves the sensitivity of muscle cells to insulin, so that insulin is able to get glucose into the muscle cells for energy. This is important if you have suffered from insulin resistance, which makes weight loss increasingly difficult. Insulin is overproduced in response to high and sustained levels of refined sugary foods. These high levels of insulin result in more triglycerides being deposited in the fat cells and in insulin resistance when the cells of the body become insensitive to insulin. When you stop eating refined sugar and start exercising, insulin metabolism is rebalanced and you are able to lose weight. It will also reduce your risk of developing type II (mature onset) diabetes.

Exercise is one of the best things you can do for your health and one of the most important reasons to exercise is that it can help you beat compulsive overeating and bulimia. Exercise is a fantastic stress buster and just a moderate increase in your level of exercise can leave you feeling calmer and in control. Whenever you feel stressed or anxious, take a long brisk walk, preferably in the countryside, and see how much better you feel afterwards. Exercise discharges the stress hormones such as cortisol that accumulate due to chronic stress. Exercise increases the flow of blood and oxygen to the brain and stimulates the release of mood-lifting endorphins that relieve pain – a natural opium known as the runner's high. These changes in brain chemistry make us feel euphoric and exhilarated. It has been shown in several studies that exercise can be as effective as antidepressants or traditional psycho-therapy in elevating mood. The more intensely you exercise, the more of these chemicals you produce, helping you to feel better and better.

It has also been shown that exercise can increase self-esteem. When we feel good about ourselves, it encourages us to take care of our health and well-being and supports us in our efforts to change. Make some form of regular exercise a priority and make time for it, because it is vital for your health and it will improve your mental outlook, mood and self-esteem – which will help you overcome compulsive eating and bulimia.

11

Love yourself better

As well as exercising to help you cope with stress, it is important to understand your emotional relationship with food and recognize your emotional triggers for overeating. It is also important to learn to control stress, anger and negative emotions so that you do not end up de-stressing with food or turning to emotional eating as a way to cope. In this chapter we will explore ways to 'love yourself better'. It is important to take care of yourself, live the life you want and to have your needs met, otherwise you end up in a cycle of depression and hopelessness, turning to food for comfort.

Discover your emotional triggers

Is it your diet or your life that's the problem? Are you struggling with past experiences? Are your life choices holding you back or contributing to the problem? Are you relating to others in an unhealthy way? Are your needs not being met? In order to start to deal with these questions, you need to understand yourself and understand the problems that are contributing to your emotional triggers for overeating. Let's start with childhood, since that is where emotional conditioning shapes our thinking and our relationship with food. Here is the list of messages we hear in childhood that we met earlier.

- We are told to eat everything on our plate and not to waste food.
- We have little control over what we eat.
- We fall into the pattern of eating certain foods established by our parents or carers.
- We end up in battles about what we eat and how much we should eat.
- We eat at preordained mealtimes, not when we are hungry.

- We are conditioned to expect food treats or sweets as a reward for good behaviour, to cheer us up or as a comfort when we are upset.
- Food is withheld as a form of punishment (no pudding if you don't eat up your dinner; no sweets if you don't behave).
- We eat the wrong foods as a form of defiance against authority.
- We see food as a treat when we are being nice to ourselves.

Challenge your thinking

The childhood messages may have become part of our subconscious thinking, but are they relevant to our lives today? The answer is, probably not. Imagine a highly successful executive, Philip Smith, sitting in a high-class London restaurant. He's dressed in a top-quality suit and is entertaining business clients, hoping to win a major sale worth millions. Next to him is his elderly mother. She's there in her working clothes and apron, just as she was when he was a child. Now imagine that the first course arrives. The conversation turns to serious business issues and everyone starts to eat the delicious starter in front of them. Philip picks up his fork and his mother immediately snatches the plate away from him. 'Philip, you mustn't eat that, you'll come out in spots. Have this instead.' He is presented with a bowl of mush, which he hates. He turns to his mother and says, 'But mum, I hate mush. Why can't I have my starter back?' She scowls at him and replies, 'Because it's good for you. Now eat it.' He scowls, but dutifully eats the mush she has presented him with, but he begins to feel nauseous since he hates the taste. He puts his fork down with food still left in the bowl. He looks across at his clients who are enjoying their starter and glancing across at Philip, rather puzzled. His mother picks up a spoon and begins to push the food towards his mouth. He turns away with his mouth clamped shut but his mother becomes stern. 'Come on, eat it all up. You can't waste good food.' Some of the mush lands on his suit jacket. Philip sullenly opens his mouth, and although he's nearly gagging on the horrible taste, he eats it all to please his mother. His business clients look on, now utterly astonished. They find it hard to believe what has just happened. Philip shrugs his shoulders and tries to explain: 'My mum always has to come with me; I just can't shake her off.' His explanation is met with stunned silence as he returns to their discussion of sales forecasts. They await the main course, the unfortunate incident apparently forgotten. When the waiters arrive, they serve a delicious dish and everyone tucks in. Philip looks across at his mother and is relieved to see her sitting quietly watching him eat. The men talk business and by the time the main course is almost over, Philip feels that he has won their interest and is confident of making a sale. He puts his cutlery down, leaving a third of his dinner on the plate. He's so excited he can't eat another thing. His mother prods him to eat the rest but he refuses, ignoring her and turning back to his clients to continue their discussion.

By the time the dessert arrives, Philip is overjoyed. He has almost clinched the sale and is feeling happy and relaxed, ready to celebrate. The waiter puts a fantastic strawberry and chocolate layer cake oozing with cream in front of him. He smiles, ready to taste the delicious-looking dessert. His mother suddenly snatches it away from him and in a determined tone says, 'Oh no you don't, my lad. You wouldn't eat all your dinner, so there's no pudding. When you finish up your veggies, you can have it then.' Philip starts to get angry and is about to throw a tantrum directed at his mother when he notices his business clients quietly muttering among themselves. He has the distinct feeling that things are not going to turn out as he hoped after all...

It's ridiculous, of course, to imagine such a scenario actually happening, but in reality we all carry around in our heads these sorts of messages from childhood, and our relationship with food becomes distorted and mixed up with our emotional reactions. Perhaps we eat up all our dinner to please our parents, and we end up overeating and feeling ashamed and out of control. Perhaps we eat in response to the emotional turmoil we are feeling about certain issues in our past. When this unhealthy reaction becomes established, it is hard to understand the original reasons for it because they have become buried in our subconscious and part of our everyday life. Sometimes we need the help of a counsellor or therapist to help us uncover

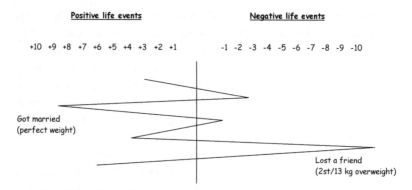

Figure 4 Plotting your life events

these triggers, but often if we can delve a little deeper into our own minds we can come up with the answer.

Try the following exercise to uncover major events in your life that may have contributed to the development of your compulsive overeating or bulimia. Copy and fill out a chart like the one in Figure 4, to plot both the positive and negative experiences that have been important to you in your life, and rate them for severity on a scale of one to ten. Also note the approximate weight you were at the time. If you can't remember, make a good guess or state whether you were satisfied or dissatisfied with your weight. This may be an indication of what triggers your overeating and your problems with food. You could also make a note of when compulsive overeating or bulimia was a particular problem and whether it was triggered by certain life events. Sometimes the reasons are far more subtle and difficult to decipher, but this is a good overview and a 'map' of your life events. It's a good starting point to see what happened when.

Have you seen any patterns arising from this exercise? Have you noted negative or positive life events that exacerbate your eating problems or a mixture of both? Is your eating ruled by reward or punishment? Is it related to certain relationships with people in your life? Have any recurring themes become apparent? When did your compulsive overeating or bulimia start and was it related to any event in particular? What was happening in your life when your eating became out of control? These sorts of questions can show up large-scale patterns and reactions in your eating behaviour, but you may need a more detailed approach in order to understand more fully the emotional reasons for overeating if they are not immediately obvious.

Look at these events again and write out the main points about each one. Ask pertinent questions: What made the event memorable and why was it rated the way it was in your diagram? Think about the people involved in each event and your relationship with them; your career and whether you were on track or frustrated with your progress. Who are the people you have a negative relationship or unresolved issues with? Who do you try to please? Who can you confide in? Who is a positive part of your life and why? Who do you admire? Who do you dislike or despise? Who do you fear? Does anyone have undue control over you? Who makes you angry? Who makes you sad? Who makes you happy? If you could change the events of the past, which ones would they be and why? How would you have preferred things to have worked out and why?

It is worth taking time to answer these questions and others that arise when you start to explore past events because this is where you will find the clues to your emotional relationship with food and your emotional triggers for overeating. Then ask two of the most important questions: What is it that triggers your emotional drive to overeat? When are you at your weakest in gaining control of your overeating? Sometimes it is simply that when we are feeling positive and in control of our lives we can resist the urge to overeat, but when we are negative and out of control we are at our most vulnerable and haven't the strength to overcome these urges. We may be reacting to childhood conditioning to reward or punish ourselves or we may overeat to comfort ourselves when we are feeling tired or out of sorts. If we can begin to decipher the reasons why we overeat and the circumstances in which we do it, then we have taken a big leap towards understanding the problem and rectifying it.

Forgiving others and yourself in order to move on

Whatever answers you have come up with as the reasons for your overeating, you may need to forgive others as well as yourself before you can move on to a healthier relationship with food. Sometimes there is no one in particular who has contributed to our problems, but it helps to develop 'forgiveness' for the events of the past. Make a list of all the people who may have contributed to the development of your emotional responses in connection with compulsive eating, whether it was parental conditioning or simply the foods you were given to eat that may have resulted in food intolerances and food addictions. It may have been nothing more than the trends in nutrition that were popular when you were growing up, such as a high-carbohydrate diet.

Now write a letter to all these people expressing forgiveness for the past. Write one to yourself too. The important thing is to find closure and be able to draw a line under the problems so that you are in a position to move on and replace negative responses with healthy ones.

Julie

Julie found it hard to find the right words to forgive. She had been brought up in a boarding school and her parents worked abroad during much of her childhood. She had fond memories of her parents but could not forgive them for sending her away to school. They were both killed in a plane crash when she was just 13 years old, and so she never did get the chance to talk to them about her compulsive eating, which developed a few years later. All through school, Julie was praised for eating the food she was given and she was disciplined not to waste food. She was very compliant in this respect – a 'good girl' for clearing her plate – and so she was frequently used as an example to the other pupils, who rebelled at mealtimes. Julie was rewarded for her good behaviour in eating everything that was put in front of her, and she became a pleaser. When her parents died, she became lonely and depressed and began to turn to food for comfort. Her overeating became out of control and she gained weight, then as she suffered the taunts of the other children at the school, she began to make herself sick after bingeing as a way of controlling her weight. Now in her 30s, Julie understands why she developed her emotional responses to food but could still not forgive her parents for sending her away to school. First Julie wrote a long letter to her teachers and carers at the school. She didn't intend to send the letter and so she vented all her anger on them for encouraging her to overeat and for the childhood conditioning that had led to her behaviour around food. When she had finished, she began to cry: she knew it was not really anyone's fault and she forgave them. They had hundreds of pupils to control and she understood why they had used her in this way. They were acting in the way they thought best at the time with no understanding of how it might affect her later in life. Then she turned her attention to her parents and realized that she understood why they sent her away to school, and that they too were acting in her best interests at the time. She knew that they loved her and wanted only the best education for her. She also managed to forgive them, knowing that if she didn't it would continue to affect her health and well-being. She decided that she had spent enough time being angry with others and that it was time to move on. She began to tackle her relationship with food in a more positive way.

Like Julie, you have to realize that by staying angry with others and yourself you are preventing your recovery and staying stuck in unhealthy emotional reactions. With the tools to stop the physical symptoms and the cravings that drive compulsive overeating and bulimia, you can also tackle the more subtle psychological aspects of the condition. You need to understand why you may have been more susceptible to overeating from both a physical and emotional perspective, forgive the past and then move on. Challenge the beliefs you had as a child since they are no longer relevant to your life as an adult. Rethink your perspective on the past and create a new canvas on which to paint the picture of you.

Loving yourself and building self-esteem

Take care of yourself and learn to be your own best friend. No one will ever be able to take care of you like you can take care of yourself, since no one can get inside your head and understand you or know what you really need. The people who are closest to you and even professional counsellors and therapists cannot know the 'real you' as you know yourself. Others can support you and help you, but ultimately *you* are the best person to understand and help *you*, and you are the only one who can take control of your eating.

Try this exercise to develop panoramic vision: imagine yourself as a child again, but see yourself from the outside as an adult would have seen you. Watch your life unfold from the outside and imagine you are your own best friend. Make a mental film of your life to date and view your entire life, remembering the traumas you went through as a child, then see the effects it had on you as an adult. Use the chart you created earlier to help you with the plot for this film. How would you have helped this person as a child and later as an adult to cope with life's problems? If you find this difficult to visualize, imagine you are trying to help a friend with similar problems to your own. How would you advise them? In other words, distance yourself from your emotional attachment to your problems and try to view them objectively. It might help to write about your problems as if you were writing to an agony aunt, then read them back and decide what you would do in your role of adviser. This is an exercise that crystallizes your thinking and helps you to look at things in a more balanced and objective way. When you have decided how you could best help this person, see if you can apply it to yourself.

Elsa

Elsa tried this exercise and realized that the abuse she'd suffered as a child was not her fault. She had been abused on several occasions by a family friend from the age of nine and had suffered in silence – her abuser had given her sweets as a reward for keeping quiet. Elsa had begun to eat compulsively during her teenage years and her weight crept up steadily. The abuse finally stopped when she was 16, but by the time she was 17 she had developed bulimia in an effort to control her overeating and as a psychological rejection of her abuser. Elsa realized that if only she had told her mother, the abuse would have stopped and she might not have suffered lasting psychological consequences. During the exercise, Elsa wrote to her 'agony aunt' with her problem, as if it were happening then. When she reversed roles and became the adviser, she told her that it was not her fault and that she should tell her mother. She gained a new perspective on her problems and was able to think more clearly about it. Elsa finally did tell her mother some 18 years after the abuse happened and felt a huge sense of relief afterwards. She also finally understood the psychological consequences of her compulsive eating and was able to forgive her abuser and move on with her life. She also keeps to a healthy diet and avoids refined sugar as she believes that she is sensitive to these foods and is at risk of food addiction. Now she is in control of her eating, has lost over four stone and is happily looking forward to her wedding day.

Dealing with anger

Sometimes we have every right to be angry, and it is a natural response when we are abused or hurt by others. But these angry feelings can sometimes be suppressed and turned inwards, resulting in detrimental consequences for ourselves and others to whom we relate. Elsa had every right to be angry with her abuser, but instead she turned her anger on to herself and developed an unhealthy relationship with food.

Recognize what or who is the cause of your anger. Try to deal with one issue at a time or you will confuse matters. Are you angry with a particular person, a situation or are you just angry at the world in general? Is your anger focused at a particular thing or an untargeted general feeling? Are you turning your anger inwards into unhealthy or even destructive behaviour? Are you blaming yourself when it is someone else's fault? Are you blaming someone else when you should address the issues and take responsibility for yourself? Are you bottling up your angry feelings or are you able to express how you feel?

Sometimes we suffer with guilt and self-blame when actually we are angry and turning this anger on to ourselves. It is important to identify why we are angry and who or what our anger is directed towards. Are you angry with yourself for allowing yourself to succumb to compulsive overeating and bulimia? If so, you are not alone, but now you know it is not your fault. The diet of modern society and the progress of civilization is to blame for the inability of modern humans to tolerate a processed and sugar-rich diet. That is most definitely not your fault. You also now have the knowledge to be able to take control of your eating. If you are angry with another person, try to decide exactly what it is you are angry about. Is it something you could talk to them about? If so, try to find a non-confrontational way to express how you feel and tell them it is important to your health that you clear up the issues you have with them. If you cannot talk to them, try sending a letter. Writing is sometimes better because you have more control over what you say and can consider the issue more carefully. It also gives the other person time to think about their response without putting them on the spot.

Sometimes when we feel unjustified anger it is a bad idea to launch into a battle with someone about your angry feelings towards them. Try going for a long walk to think it over and calm down before you confront someone. You'll be surprised how often a walk can moderate your feelings and help you avoid arguments and stress. It is an effective way to count to ten!

Sometimes anger is diffuse and unfocused. We know something is making us unhappy and angry but we can't identify a cause. Sometimes we suffer with a chronic underlying resentment towards others when really the problem is that we are not fulfilling our own dreams.

Jane

Jane was deeply unhappy. She had been for the past five years and couldn't really understand why. Her life was like a storybook. She had a loving husband, the perfect home and a beautiful six-year-old daughter. She spent her days at home taking care of the house and family and helping her husband with his PR company. Everyone told her how lucky she was; yet despite her idyllic lifestyle, she was hiding a problem that was getting out of hand – bulimia. Jane confided in a friend one day and as she talked about her problems, the reason for her unhappiness became clear. Jane had wanted to go to art college and become a professional artist, but when her daughter was born she had put all her dreams on hold. She felt a chronic resentment at her family for this and yet she couldn't bring herself to express how she felt. She had turned her anger upon herself by overeating. She developed bulimia as a way of controlling her eating and almost as a self-punishment. Jane's friend urged her to talk to her husband and explain how she felt. Two weeks later, Jane spoke to her husband about her unhappiness at not being able to go to art college, although she didn't tell him about her eating problems. She was surprised at how understanding he was and suggested they employ someone to help with the company while she went to college to fulfil her dream. Jane is now in her second year of an art degree and her eating problems are under control. She is happier than she has ever been and has re-found the love she had for her family.

Becoming assertive

Being assertive is a healthy attitude to have. It is not aggressive and not submissive, but it means standing up for your rights and needs without violating those of others. It is the ideal position to be in in most situations and allows you to say 'no' to unreasonable requests so that you can manage your time effectively. Your position with others is dynamic and the reactions of others often depend on the situation and on their own communication skills, but being assertive leads to high self-esteem, increased confidence and improved communication. By increasing your self-esteem and your confidence you are likely to take more initiatives and improve your chances of success in making the desired changes in your life.

Both aggressive and non-assertive or submissive behaviour often originate from low self-esteem. Self-esteem is your own evaluation of yourself, of your worth as a person and your beliefs about yourself as a competent, worthwhile human being. Aggressive behaviour in people may give the impression of overconfidence and self-assuredness but can be a veil to cover up insecurity and a poor self-regard. When you act in a submissive or non-assertive way, you use a lot of nervous energy by worrying about upsetting others. You can save yourself all that by being more assertive.

Making positive changes to your life will naturally increase your self-esteem and your confidence, but here are some examples of specific ways you can alter your behaviour in order to become more assertive:

- Use brief statements and get to the point. Avoid long rambling speeches that cause confusion. Be clear about what you want.
- Avoid justifications such as, 'I wouldn't normally do this but ...' They tend to weaken your argument.
- Don't apologize profusely before you ask for something ('I'm terribly sorry to bother you ...'). This also weakens your position. You don't need to seek permission to ask for what you want.
- Find out how your plans fit in with others by asking questions. Find out what something involves before you agree to it.
- Give yourself time to consider requests when not under pressure. Get into the habit of saying, 'Let me think about it' or 'I'm not sure. I'll get back to you.'
- Don't dismiss yourself by saying things like, 'I could do with some help with this but it's OK, I'll manage ...' This just invites people to ignore your needs.
- Don't put yourself down by saying things like, 'I'm hopeless at

this ...' This weakens your position and is a dead giveaway for low self-esteem and lack of assertiveness.

- Avoid statements or questions that come across as threatening or overbearing, such as, 'That's useless: it will never work' or 'Why on earth did you do *that* ?' They come across as controlling and aggressive.
- Avoid sarcasm or put-downs.
- Use steady eye contact to reinforce your point. Submissive people often avoid eye contact and inadvertently give the other person control of the situation, while aggressive people tend to stare at their opponent and dominate.
- Use open body language and sit or stand in a relaxed posture with head held up. Avoid nervous movements such as hand wringing or folded arms. Submissive people tend to curl up to protect themselves; assertive people stand up and face the world; and aggressive people lean forward and attack.
- Find inventive ways around problems and obstacles.

Above all, to behave in an assertive manner it helps to have solid goals and a plan that you are deeply committed to and passionate about. That way, you have something to stand up for and will be far less likely to submit to the will of others.

12

Dealing with social situations

Being assertive about your eating in social situations is vital if you are to achieve your goal of overcoming compulsive eating and bulimia. You have probably been withdrawing from social activities for a long time, but you no longer have to let compulsive eating and bulimia rule your life. Once you have taken control of food intolerances and food addictions, you are in a position to make considered choices about the foods you eat, and it is vital that you do not eat your trigger foods again if you want to avoid a relapse. It's the same for smokers, alcoholics and drug addicts with their particular addictive substances. Unless you want to withdraw from social activities for ever, you *have* to find a way to cope and be able to refuse to eat the foods that are causing you problems. Just one slip because you are too polite to say anything could set you off again into a cycle of compulsive overeating and bulimia. Once you have broken the cycle, you do not want to end up back on that roller coaster again.

So why do we feel obliged to eat food we don't want at social events when it could cause us so much distress and misery afterwards? Usually we just don't want to make a fuss and to fit in with everyone else, sometimes we have a need to please people or we are trying to hide the problems we have around food. Often we use social activities as the perfect excuse to overindulge, and yet we feel guilty and depressed afterwards.

All this can be cured by being assertive and treating your eating problems seriously. Other people who do not suffer do not understand how detrimental it is to you to eat your trigger foods, and they do not have the background knowledge you have about our physiology to understand the problem. It's all very well for people to take a flippant attitude and say, 'Surely one little slice of pizza won't hurt?' or 'Go on: you have to have some birthday cake.' But these small amounts are all it takes to set you off on the road to bingeing again and it could mean destroying weeks of hard-won control over your eating. While your host is getting on with their life normally after the party, you could be suffering months of being out of control with your eating and coping with a spiral of depression and misery. That is most definitely not worth a taste of pizza or cake. If you had an allergy to a particular food that could literally kill you, you wouldn't hesitate to tell people you couldn't eat it and no one would dream of forcing you to – so why must food intolerances and food addictions be any different? Although they may not kill you, they cause chronic suffering over many years and sometimes over a whole lifetime. They can cause untold emotional suffering as well as that huge list of such physical symptoms as digestive problems, headaches and fatigue. Don't let anyone persuade you that you should eat something that causes you all these problems. It's like letting a heroin dealer persuade you to take heroin so that you become hooked. Treat it as seriously as this if you want to stay in control and look after yourself. No one else can do it for you.

Another thing to think about is that perhaps many others at social gatherings are also food addicts and even perhaps compulsive eaters or bulimics themselves. It is hard to quantify how many there are, so in a large social gathering you may not be the only one with an eating problem. When you see everyone else tucking in to forbidden foods, perhaps food is controlling their lives and they would give anything to be free, as you will be when you start putting your plan into action. Learn to look at the problem objectively and from the 'outside'.

The main thing is not worry about what everyone else is doing. You don't have to eat unsuitable food just because everyone else does. Take a stand. Do you really believe that other people care in the least about what you are eating? Did they care that food was controlling your life? Did they even know? What I am saying is that most people are too busy with their own concerns and what they are eating themselves to be worried about or even notice what you are doing. I bet you could go to a buffet party, put some food on your plate and walk around with it all night, not eating a single morsel, and no one would even notice. I'm not suggesting you don't eat anything, but if you know in advance that all that will be on offer are all the wrong foods for you, why not eat before you leave home and don't eat at the party? You could even put some fruit or nuts in your bag to nibble on while everyone else poisons their bodies with processed foods! Start to feel wholly justified in what you are doing with your new eating plan. It will give you strength to stick to it.

One solution is to tell people about the problems you have with food, and that you can't eat certain trigger foods. However, there is no need to explain, and you shouldn't really have to do so unless you want to. There are several ways to approach being able to eat or not eat the foods you want to without feeling obliged or pressured. Here are some more ideas to help you cope with eating and social occasions.

- Be assertive. No one should feel entitled to dictate to you what you should eat. Calmly and firmly stand your ground and refuse to eat anything you do not want or that you know will cause you problems. You have every right to eat the foods you want to, so don't feel obliged or pressured in social situations.
- Don't feel controlled as a result of childhood conditioning. If you find yourself 'eating all your dinner' automatically, stop and think. If it seems like some old message replaying itself you do not have to respond; you do not have to please people by overeating. Simply be aware of why you are behaving the way you are with food and make a logical and objective decision about it.
- Just say you are not hungry or that you overate at lunchtime and you couldn't eat another thing.
- Say that a particular food doesn't agree with you. No need for lengthy explanations: just make it known that you can't eat something you know is a trigger food for you. We all have food preferences; no one needs to know why you can't eat it – you just can't and that's that.
- Say you've had a tummy upset recently and you don't want to aggravate it again. No one will force food on you if it could make you ill. Just eat the foods you can eat without problems.
- Tell people you are on a new healthy eating plan and refuse processed and sugary foods that you know are a problem for you. Most people will admire you for taking up healthy eating and wish they could be as disciplined about it themselves.

- People respect vegetarians for their diet choices. Why shouldn't they respect your diet choices too?
- People respect the diets of other cultures. Why shouldn't they respect yours?
- If it is a dinner party, try to warn your hosts in advance about the food you cannot eat. That way you won't be caught out and can make sure your needs are met. Your hosts will undoubtedly be glad to know they can accommodate your dietary needs.
- Carry some fresh fruit and nuts with you as an alternative when everyone else is having processed fast food and burgers.
- Remember that the people who care about you will do whatever they can to accommodate your new food tastes.

Once you get used to stating your wishes concerning food, it will become automatic and people will come to know what you will and will not eat. You may be surprised at how easy it is to follow your wishes in this respect. Sometimes, as with anyone else following a particular diet, you will not have much choice and will have to do the best you can with what is available. When you are in a restaurant that is not serving the fresh natural foods you want, just avoid your trigger foods. Give the chips a miss and go for a baked potato instead; go for the fish or steak rather than the pasta, and always look for the best option that will fit in with your new way of eating.

Taking responsibility for you

No one can do it for you. The only person who can control your eating is you. Unless you take action to address your problems, things will stay the same. It is the same for other addicts: smokers, alcoholics and drug users have to take responsibility and give up for themselves, and food addicts also have to take action if they want things to change. You already know this, and the fact that you are reading this book shows that you want to conquer your problems with food. But sometimes there are subtle reasons why we continue with bad habits and destructive behaviour, despite wanting to change. Sometimes there are hidden rewards for our behaviour that are buried in our subconscious and need a little prod to come to light. Think about the rewards of continuing with your compulsive eating and bulimia and scrutinize them to see if they really are worth all the misery. Are you trying to gain approval or trying to please people by overeating? This can happen when we are responding to childhood conditioning to 'eat up all your dinner like a good girl/boy'. If we hear this message often enough, and especially when it is reinforced with other rewards, we end up overeating. The problem is that in our subconscious we are still trying to please and gain approval. This behaviour is no longer relevant to your adult life, and simply being aware of it can help you overcome the impulse to eat in order to please people. Remember how ridiculous Philip looked in front of his business clients when he ate up all his mush just to please his mother? Imagine you are in a similar situation in your adult life. Do you still have a parent sitting next to you at every mealtime? If so, it's time to let go of these old messages. Take responsibility for what you eat. No one but you should be deciding what you put into your body. Would you tell another adult what they should eat? Of course not! It would be rude and disrespectful to dictate to someone about what they should eat, so don't let anyone try to do it to you.

Listen to your internal dialogue

Learn to identify the conversations that go on in your head concerning food. We all have conflicting thoughts and emotions concerning food. Here are some you may recognize, along with some other things to consider:

• I'm going out tonight so the diet starts tomorrow.

When you keep putting it off, tomorrow never comes. Before you know it, another year has gone by and you've done nothing to help yourself get control of your overeating. When you are out, you can still make choices about what you eat. Skip the chips and the dessert and choose the healthy options instead.

• I shouldn't eat it but I can't be rude and not have some of Aunt Mabel's homemade cake.

If Aunt Mabel knew of the heartache you went through concerning food, she'd understand. If people love you and care about your health and well-being, they won't force food on you. Give people a chance to show they care.

- I know it's fattening but I mustn't waste perfectly good food.

So how does your being overweight and out of control around food help? It is far better for that food to end up in the bin (or in the dog) than on your hips. Challenge your parental conditioning and change your thinking.

- I know I'm on a diet but I've had a hard day at work; I deserve a chocolate bar.

Why does the reward have to be food-related? Why not get a massage or have a nice long soak in the bath with your favourite music? It's not rewarding to be a slave to food.

- I'm on holiday; I can't miss the opportunity to try the local cuisine.

You may also jeopardize your chance of regaining control too. Do you want to get over your compulsive eating or forever find more excuses not to get on top of it?

- Surely just one slice of cake can't hurt?

It could do immeasurable harm. We have already discovered why refined sugar is contributing to the problem. If you are an addict, you must stay away from the substances causing the addiction – one mouthful is all it need take to trigger off your compulsive overeating or bulimia again. Beware.

- Everyone else is tucking in, why should I miss out?

Well, life isn't fair! And have you considered the possibility that many of those other people also have food addictions? I bet they would love to have the means to gain control and be free too if they only knew how.

- I went for a walk today so I've earned it.

We have already discovered that exercise is not a strategy for weight loss.

- I'm tired and haven't the energy to worry about what I eat today.

When you are tired you are vulnerable to compulsive eating, so it is imperative that you stop and think about the consequences and eat something wholesome instead.

- I'm in a hurry so I'll just have to grab something from the bakery.

It's just as quick to grab an apple, a banana, a natural yoghurt, a packet of natural unsalted nuts or some cooked meat. A quick snack doesn't have to be processed food, and if you always keep a bag of natural snacks handy you won't even have to nip to the shops when you're in a rush.

- But I want it really badly.

You are craving this food because of food intolerances and addictions. If it is a problem food then you must resist it, as any ex-smoker, ex-alcoholic or ex-drug addict will tell you. You already know the consequences of triggering compulsive overeating and bulimia. Do you really want to go back to that? It is entirely up to you ...

Turn negatives into positives. Develop a positive mental attitude around food and your eating habits. Believe that your new way of eating is the best thing you can do for your health and to enable you to overcome your eating problems. Challenge your beliefs about your eating and your food choices. Many of our eating habits are based on old patterns developed in childhood and have no place in our adult lives when we can choose for ourselves what we can eat. Celebrate the fact that you are able to eat whatever you want to, and choose to break free of food addictions, take control of your eating problems and make logical, objective choices about your diet based on what you need – not on cultural norms or the food choices of other people.

Live the life you want

Have a purpose in life. Too often we spend our time in pointless activities and end up bored, dissatisfied and unfulfilled. No wonder we turn to food for comfort. When your life has meaning and you feel happy and satisfied that you are striving to reach your full potential, your focus changes. Jane found that her problems around food disappeared when she took the decision to go to art college and began to strive to reach her dream of becoming a professional artist. It is your life, and if you are unhappy and turning to food for comfort, then maybe you are not living the life you want. Are you living your life to please others or fit in with their expectations? Are you putting your dreams on hold for others but secretly feeling resentful? This is a recipe for disaster as far as your problems with food are concerned. Are you going to spend more years of your life suffering in silence and turning to food to make you feel temporarily better? Life is precious and far too short for that, and you deserve better.

Maybe you have spent so long being unhappy and unfulfilled that you don't even know what it is you want out of life. If so, try making a list of all the things you'd like to try and all the things you'd like to be, however outlandish or silly they may seem to you. No one will see this list except you. Now imagine that you won the lottery – millions of pounds – so that you could do whatever you wanted. What would you choose? Would you change jobs, give up work, start your own business, buy a new house? Think how your life would change if you had all the money you ever needed. Now think about what you'd do with your life if you only had a year to live. What would you simply have to fit in from your list? Write it all down. Now look at your list and see what you can do right now to make those things happen. What is holding you back? What can you do to overcome these barriers? Too often we postpone making changes we know we have to make to our lives, but the reality is that life slips away too quickly. Don't end up on your deathbed wishing you'd taken action to achieve the things you know you are capable of. Make a start and do it now.

Sadie

Sadie was deeply unhappy with her marriage, and although she loved them she felt trapped as a mother of three young children. Her best friend Laura had been trying to convince her to leave her husband for several years but Sadie felt unable to. The two friends had often discussed starting a business together but Sadie couldn't see how this was possible with her family commitments and a sullen, disapproving husband. She felt trapped and had turned to food as a comfort, and her weight was escalating alarmingly. One day while shopping she saw her husband with another woman. They were obviously an item by the way they were touching each other and Sadie was distraught. She knew deep down that something was very wrong but had not really considered that her husband was being unfaithful. Later that day, when she had calmed down a little, she spoke to him about it and he confessed to having had an affair for the past two years. After much discussion, arguments and tears, her husband left her for the other woman. Sadie went though six months of depression and readjustment, and all the while her eating problems became worse and she was feeling ill and tired all the time. Her friend Laura was deeply concerned about her. Sadie was finding it hard to manage financially, and one day decided she had nothing to lose by starting the business she and Laura had talked about for so long. They approached a bank, succeeded in getting a loan and opened their own private nursery school. The first eight months were hard, but gradually they built a good reputation in the neighbourhood and more and more parents sent their children to the school. Sadie was happier than she had been in a long time and felt that she was finally taking control of her life. She also managed to take control of her eating and has kept this up for over five months. She feels she is on the road to recovery, especially since she has also changed her diet and is eating healthy natural foods.

Sadie's traumatic situation prompted her to change her life and take control. It was the best thing that could have happened to her. Are you waiting for life to take a downward turn before you change things, or will you start to make those changes now?

Get your needs met

Are you getting what you need from other people or are you continually behaving like a doormat and being walked all over? When you allow others to treat you with disrespect, or take you for granted, you are saying that you don't matter and that other people's needs are more important than yours. Absolutely not true! Your needs and wants are as equally important as everyone else's on the planet, whoever they are! When you allow yourself to be less important than anyone else, you end up being used more often than not, which is not healthy for you or the other people involved. When this situation continues for any length of time you end up feeling resentful and find yourself pulling away from people. When you have problems around food it also inevitably exacerbates these problems too. You owe it to yourself and your physical and emotional health to develop self-esteem and realize that you are as important as everyone else and that your needs and wants are as important as theirs. Learn to ask for what you want, especially from the people you live with. When you have been subservient for years it can seem strange to start asking that your needs be taken into account, but you owe it to yourself in the interests of your health, getting in control of your eating, and in order to build better relationships with the significant people in your life. If you find it difficult to ask for what you want, why not try a message board where you can write down things you need or want others to do for you. Perhaps they can also use it to send messages to you as a way of ensuring everyone's needs are met. Ask for things like a little more help around the house and for emotional needs like, 'I need more cuddles!' A message board is a safe way to ask without getting into long discussions or confrontations. You could also try writing letters to ask for what you need or to explain emotional issues that you find difficult. Letters can form the basis of further discussion if you want them to.

Other coping strategies

You might find it helpful to keep a food and feelings diary until your new diet becomes an engrained habit, which can take several months. Make a note of what you eat and of your feelings and how your life is going day by day. This will highlight any associations with your emotional eating patterns. Make a list of foods you can eat freely and put it on the wall in the kitchen. Write out some recipes and ideas for meals so that you're not stumped when you're in a hurry and tempted to grab anything. Always have plenty of 'instant' snacks available, such as apples, bananas, strawberries, grapes, nuts and seeds. Even a packet of cooked ham or other cold meat or some cheese is better to snack on than the usual crisps and processed foods that can cause problems for you.

Don't shop for food when you are hungry – that's asking for trouble! Make a list and stick to it, so that you plan in advance what you will eat. Don't shop when you are tired, stressed or feeling upset or angry either – this is when you are most likely to be tempted to use food as an emotional comfort. You could try shopping over the internet so that you can plan your meals and not be subject to impulse buying.

When you are eating, eat slowly. Savour every mouthful, really enjoy every morsel and concentrate on what you are eating. It is easy to overeat when your attention is distracted by the TV. Notice when your hunger is satisfied. Often we blithely continue to overeat even though our hunger has been satisfied. To help you avoid this, try serving yourself smaller portions. It will help you feel less deprived if you use smaller plates for this. If at the end of a meal you still feel hungry, wait 20 minutes and see how you feel then. It can take this long for your hunger satiation signals to kick in. Make an occasion of every meal instead of grabbing something quickly as you fly through the kitchen. Begin to enjoy cooking interesting and wholesome meals, knowing you are nourishing your body. Work on making them look attractive on the plate and take a pride in what you eat. How about growing your own fruit and vegetables? It's much cheaper and there is nothing finer than freshly picked veggies from the garden. You also know they are fresh, not genetically modified, and you may even have grown them organically. If you have a surplus, you could freeze them to see you through the winter months. It's good fun when you get into the habit!

Drink plenty of water too to stay hydrated and to help fill you up. A large glass of water before a meal can help reduce the amount of food you eat. Fill up on fibre-rich vegetables and appetite-satisfying protein foods. Remember that the nutrient-dense foods you will be eating – the fruit, vegetables, meat and fish – will satisfy your body much better than processed nutrient-poor foods. Once you get into the habit of eating natural foods you will find that your appetite will regulate itself much better.

After a few months your body will be well nourished and you will feel even more in control of your eating because your body will not be craving the nutrients it needs (and hasn't been getting) any more. You will be giving it the right ingredients it was designed to use for energy, repair and making new tissue. You will notice a shine on your hair, your skin will be clearer and you will be full of energy and vitality, just as you are meant to be. Your brain will be sharp and alert and your body will be functioning efficiently, as it is meant to. These changes don't happen overnight, so be patient and give your body a chance to heal from all the abuse it's had to take over the years with the wrong fuel. A car engine would seize up if you put the wrong petrol into it. Your body is also trying to recover, so give it a fair chance.

Coping with stress

Stress for our ancestors was a survival mechanism. The stress response evolved as a way to respond to threats such as predators – the flight-or-fight response. The physiological pathway by which stressful stimuli produce the stress hormone cortisol is shown in Figure 5. Stress signals from various parts of the brain (including emotional stress signals) and sensory receptors in the body are sent to the hypothalamus at the base of the brain. The hypothalamus releases a hormone called corticotrophin-releasing hormone. This in turn stimulates the pituitary gland, which lies just below the hypothalamus, to produce another hormone called adrenocorticotrophic hormone, or ACTH. ACTH in turn stimulates the adrenal cortex in the adrenal glands situated above the kidneys, and this is where the stress hormone cortisol is released. The release of cortisol into the bloodstream:

1 stimulates the catabolism (breakdown) of protein that the body can use for energy;
2 stimulates the uptake of amino acids (from the catabolism of protein) into the liver for conversion to glucose for energy for the brain, heart and muscles;
3 inhibits the uptake of glucose in many body cells to allow energy to be used for vital organs.

This gives the body a surge of energy for the flight-or-fight response and also increases the protein available to repair tissues in case of injury. The body is put on alert: hearing and sense of smell become more acute; muscles tense ready for activity; heart and breathing rates increase; blood pressure elevates and blood flow is diverted to the brain and muscles at the expense of the skin and internal organs, ready for action. This sudden release of cortisol is designed

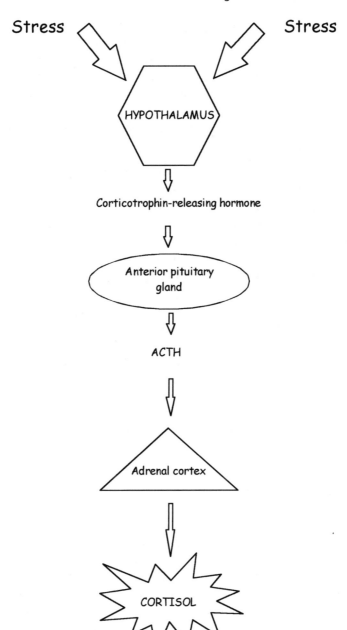

Figure 5 How stress produces the stress hormone cortisol

for a quick response to danger, and once the cortisol is used up by running or fighting, the body quickly returns to normal.

However, problems occur when we do not use up the excess cortisol and discharge it from our bodies. People who are able to deal quickly with stress have the lowest risk of health problems associated with increased cortisol levels, but those who build up chronic stress and fail to deal with it effectively are at risk from a multitude of conditions, such as:

- heart disease resulting from the increased 'bad' cholesterol levels (low density lipoproteins – LDLs) caused by the release of fatty acids into the bloodstream by the liver;
- damage to the heart muscle itself and arrhythmias from constantly elevated levels of stress hormones;
- irreversible destruction of brain cells due to surges in cortisol;
- muscle spasms and tension, causing back pain, stiff aching limbs and headaches;
- increased cortisol interference with glucose metabolism, increasing the risks of heart disease, stroke, cataracts, diabetes, obesity, insulin resistance and premature ageing;
- pressure on the immune system, which can result in a lowered resistance to infections such as colds, flu, asthma, allergies and other infections;
- lowering of our emotional strength to cope with life, and increased vulnerability to anxiety, depression and – importantly – eating disorders.

Chronic stress that is not dealt with can cause untold damage to your physical and emotional health, and also dampens your spirit for life.

We were genetically evolved to balance stressful periods of hunting and dealing with wild predators with periods of relaxation and socializing. Our ancestors were also living amid nature, with green grass, trees and plants, clean water and pure air – not having to contend with miles upon miles of barren concrete and the polluted atmosphere of our modern towns and cities. It is so important to reconnect with nature on a regular basis if we are to experience balance and harmony and beat the stresses of modern life. A long walk in the country or along the beach can do wonders for your soul as well as your physical and emotional health.

Are you a constant worrier? This is so damaging to your health and leads to chronic stress. Begin to worry less about things you can't change and actually do something about the things you can change – and know the difference! If you are feeling pressured and stressed, take time out for a brisk walk to discharge the excess cortisol in your body or have it out with whoever is adding to your stress – then quickly forget it and get on with your day. Chronic resentment and grumbling anger seething away below the surface is a major cause of chronic stress, so deal with it and get it out of the way.

Make sure you cope with stress and try to balance your life. Too much work and not enough relaxation is not good for you; neither is not having enough stimulation or projects that challenge you. Use exercise as a way to de-stress, and get some time to yourself to think and just *be*. It is important to spend time alone in contemplation. Try meditation and yoga to cope with stress and to balance your body. It is a great way to get into control again. There are plenty of good books on meditation and there may be some meditation or yoga classes in your area that you could try.

Break the cycle of stress:

- Maybe you need to delegate more, take on less, or re-evaluate your relationships at home or at work. Are you really happy with the direction your life is taking? If not, it's up to you to do something about it.
- Manage your time effectively. Is what you are doing both urgent and important? Can you delegate some tasks to others or plan them in for a less hectic time? Many everyday tasks can be unceremoniously dumped!
- Set priorities. Is your life cluttered up with 'stuff to do'? Discover what's really important and realize that you can't do everything and be all things to all people. You're a human being, not a machine. Don't spend time with people you don't like or can't get on with, and make your time the precious priority that it is.
- Let others take responsibility for themselves. Are you always picking up after the kids and running errands for others? Let them do it themselves.
- Spend more time with the people and the pets you love. Organize romantic evenings with your loved one and make time to catch

up with friends and family. Spend time playing with the cats or walking the dog. It all helps to release stress.

- Take stress seriously. You have seen what damage it can cause your body. It is vital that you tackle the causes of stress in your life, for your physical and emotional health and to help you get in control of problems around food.
- Set aside some time every day for formal relaxation. Yoga and meditation are both good choices.
- Get active. Even a five-minute walk can help reduce cortisol levels.
- Have a long soak in a bubble bath and spoil yourself with some scented candles and body lotion. Take deep breaths and feel calm again.
- Invest in a massager to help de-stress your aching muscles after a long hard day.
- Have a good long belly laugh every day! Laughter really is the best medicine. Think positive thoughts and be optimistic for the future. A negative attitude and negative people will drag you down and are an endless source of stress. Make up your mind to develop a positive frame of mind and look for the good in everything.

Getting enough sleep

Research from the USA shows that a lack of sleep disrupts a series of metabolic and hormonal processes that help to control appetite. For example, levels of the hormone leptin, which plays an important role in signalling to your brain that you've eaten enough, are reduced by sleep deprivation. Shift workers are particularly at risk and tend to eat more in order to stay awake.

Sleep deprivation has similar effects on the body as stress and can lead to weight gain, increased cortisol levels and a disruption to the insulin–glucose mechanism, leading to insulin resistance and the risk of diabetes. Sleep deprivation also leads to irritability, low motivation, poor memory and concentration, and depression. It interferes with your immune system, making you more susceptible to infection and prolonging recovery from illness or injury.

Lack of sleep reduces the body's ability to repair itself and recover from wear and tear. It is during sleep that most of the repair of organs and tissues takes place and growth hormone is released. Our ancestors went to sleep with the sunset and awoke with the light of dawn. They lived to the rhythm of nature. Now we have artificial light and plenty of entertainment during the hours of darkness, so that we are going against our natural instincts to sleep when it gets dark. When people take part in experiments and are placed in a room without clocks, they tend to sleep more than they normally would, showing that we don't generally get enough sleep. It is important that you make sure you are getting good quality sleep; seven to eight hours in a 24-hour period. If you are becoming stressed or have a demanding schedule at work or at home – or are trying to cope with relationship problems, parenting problems or any number of demands that life makes on you without enough sleep – it is tempting to return to your old habits of turning to food for comfort. This, as you know, will be totally counterproductive and may set you right back to square one.

Try the following to ensure you are getting enough quality sleep:

- Try and get an early night at least three times a week.
- Take a long walk in the fresh air every day if you can, to encourage restful natural sleep.
- Sleep on in the mornings when you can, perhaps at the weekends.
- Take naps when you can, maybe during your lunch break – but not later in the day as this will prevent you sleeping soundly at night.
- If you work night shifts, make sure you catch up with your sleep the next day.
- Avoid stimulants such as caffeine, nicotine and alcohol before bedtime.
- Make sure you have a warm, cosy, comfortable bed.
- Try to have as much quiet as possible. Use earplugs if necessary.
- Get lots of fresh air and sunshine to enable you to sleep soundly and cope better with stress. Spend time in nature as our ancestors did.
- Make sure your bedroom is well ventilated.

- Have a bedtime ritual, such as a bath, to help you relax and let your body know it's time for sleep.
- If you have trouble sleeping, don't lie there forcing yourself to go to sleep. Get up and read a book or do something that will relax you, and try again when you feel sleepy.

Use your imagination

Try visualizations to prime your brain for the changes you want to make. Close your eyes and imagine yourself as you want to be – slim, fit, successful and in control of your eating. You could make audio tapes with positive suggestions for change. Play them while you relax or sleep to get the message deeply embedded in your subconscious.

Your imagination is a powerful ally when it comes to making changes in your life. Rehearse in your mind the way you want to be in the future and practise how you will achieve it. Athletes use these visualization techniques before a race, to see themselves crossing the finishing line for example, or golfers for getting a hole-in-one. You can do this too with your goals to overcome compulsive eating and bulimia. Imagine yourself succeeding, and your subconscious will strive to create your vision in reality.

The new you!

Once you are ready to make a start and you have set the date for the week when you finally take control of your eating, plan a change of image. Try a new hairstyle or have a complete makeover, but mark the occasion somehow with a 'new you'. How about a party to celebrate the start of your new life as an ex-compulsive eater or bulimic? Use it as a good way to get rid of all the white flour and sugar lurking in your cupboards! The main thing is to mark the occasion somehow and celebrate the positive steps you are taking. Good luck!

Conclusion

To summarize, the steps you need to take to gain control of compulsive overeating and bulimia, stay in control and love yourself better, are:

- Prepare to change.
- Take control by cutting out all substances that cause food cravings. Substitute unhealthy foods for natural, healthy ones.
- Think straight, free of food cravings, and plan how you will manage your lifetime diet.
- Choose your treats carefully and plan how you will incorporate them into your diet using the 80:20 or the 90:10 rule, and avoid your trigger foods.
- Treat your problems with food as seriously as any alcoholic, smoker or drug addict should if they are to overcome their problems with addictive substances.
- Use exercise as a road to physical and emotional health.
- Love yourself better and address emotional issues that contribute to the problem.
- Learn to cope effectively with stress.
- Find purpose in your life.
- Remember that you are an ex-compulsive eater. There is no permanent 'cure' that allows you to eat indiscriminately.

Being an ex-compulsive eater

Be aware that you are an ex-compulsive eater or bulimic. Sadly there is no 'cure' that allows you to continue to eat indiscriminately and remain in control. There are certain food triggers that may always set you off bingeing, and these must be avoided at all costs. It may be possible in the future to have small amounts of problem foods on rare occasions without harm, but always be aware of the risk you take and how easy it would be to lapse into compulsive overeating again. Once you have control and the substances in your problem food are out of your system, you must give your body a rest from them. You wouldn't expect a heavy smoker to be able to smoke even one cigarette and not become addicted again within days of giving up, so don't expect this of yourself. You are addicted to certain foods and you must be aware of this and avoid them completely. It may be that you can never eat these foods again – life isn't fair! There are probably many ex-smokers, ex-alcoholics and ex-drug addicts who dream of having a fix of their particular addictive substance but wouldn't dare because of the dire consequences: you are not alone. But there are so many fabulous food alternatives you can enjoy and not get into trouble with, which other types of addicts do not have. After at least four months, try a little experiment if you wish. If you haven't eaten wheat products for four months, try a few slices of bread or some pasta, but keep the rest of your diet the same. By introducing one food at a time, you can monitor your reaction to it and make an objective decision as to whether you want to risk eating this food in moderation again. Try this for other banned foods that you enjoy. You may decide to introduce them as treats in your 80:20 rule if they do not cause you problems. Just be careful...

Finding support

You are not alone with compulsive eating and bulimia. There are many others out there who understand the problems you are having and who can support you and help you through it all. Reach out and get the help you need, and approach a trusted friend or someone in your family to confide in. Eating disorders isolate people, and those who have them can feel lonely struggling with their problems. People will understand when you go to them for support. If they love you and care about you they will do whatever they can to help you through it – you do not have to be alone.

I wish you all the best for your journey back to health. I promise that your life will improve dramatically once you take control and free yourself of food intolerances and food addictions. Don't let food control your life a day longer!

Recipe suggestions

These suggestions for recipes for natural health are quick and easy, with no weighing or exotic ingredients. They are simple and healthy meals you can prepare for yourself and your family.

Starters and snacks

Stuffed mushrooms Large open-cap mushrooms topped with slices of cheese and baked in the oven.

Creamy potato-stuffed mushrooms Mushrooms stuffed with mashed potatoes mixed with cooked bacon bits, flaked fish or crunchy chopped vegetables according to taste, baked in the oven, and garnished with chives or a sprig of parsley.

Wicked orange cups Cut an orange in half (horizontally) and scrape out the flesh to leave two 'cups'. Chop the orange flesh and mix with chopped apple, chopped walnuts and a little dark rum. Leave to marinade in the fridge, and enjoy!

Celery sticks Prepare some celery sticks and cut to desired length. Lay on a baking sheet and crumble strong cheese, such as Stilton or mature Cheddar, along the hollow length and grill until the cheese has melted. Can be served with crunchy potato wedges.

Crunchy potato wedges Unpeeled potatoes, chopped into wedge shapes, parboiled, then brushed with olive oil and baked. (Top with grated cheese for cheesy potato wedges.)

Salmon and apple salad Tinned or fresh cooked salmon mixed with chopped apple and walnuts, served on fresh watercress, garnished with chopped chives or a squeeze of lemon juice.

Grapefruit and cheese salad Grapefruit segments and cubes of your favourite cheese, with watercress or a side salad. Also delicious with apples, mandarins or oranges instead of grapefruit.

Omelettes These offer so many possibilities – prawn, sweetcorn, peas, diced cooked potatoes, mixed peppers or mushrooms.

Nibbles

- Mixed nuts and raisins;
- Sunflower or pumpkin seeds;
- Raw carrots;
- Celery and cheese;
- An apple and some cheese;
- A piece of fruit: an apple, pear, grapes, strawberries or a banana;
- An apple and a carrot chopped into a bowl with a handful of nuts and raisins;
- Dried seaweed sprinkled over a variety of dishes as a tasty and healthy garnish.

Main meals

Meat kebabs and rice Your favourite meat skewered with chopped peppers and mushrooms and baked in the oven, with brown rice. For a special treat, add sweet chilli or barbecue sauce to the kebabs for the last couple of minutes of cooking. Add vegetables if liked.

Liver and bacon Fried liver, onions and bacon in olive oil, adding seasoning to taste and served with fresh vegetables.

Chicken or turkey stir-fry Diced free-range chicken or turkey stir-fried, with stir-fried vegetables and brown rice.

Steak and Stilton Lean steak grilled, sprinkled with grated Stilton and served with a baked potato, a knob of butter and fresh vegetables.

Fish in white wine Fish such as sole, cod, haddock or plaice poached in white wine, garlic and onion and served with fresh green vegetables.

Chilli and baked potato Baked potato topped with lean minced beef simmered with onions, sliced mushrooms and finely chopped chilli peppers, and chilli powder to taste.

Ginger chicken Chicken breast fried with onion, garlic, chopped peppers and mushrooms; then simmered with a teaspoon of powdered ginger and chicken broth or water and served with fresh vegetables.

Pork chops and salad Grilled pork chops, served with apple and walnut salad. Add a baked potato if liked. Try marinating the chops in a delicious mixture of orange juice and rum (or wine) too, then grill the chops, and heat the marinade in a small saucepan to pour over them to serve.

Turkey cheese pockets Turkey breast sliced along the side and the pocket filled with your favourite cheese and some herbs, such as sage or thyme if liked; then wrap in bacon rashers and roast in the oven. Serve with salad or vegetables.

Baked fish Any fresh fish such as cod, haddock, salmon, trout, halibut, or flatfish such as plaice or flounder, is delicious wrapped in foil and baked in the oven. Try adding some parsley or dill, lemon or lime juice and a drizzle of olive oil. Serve with fresh vegetables and maybe a sprinkle of black pepper.

Tinned salmon or tuna Makes an instant meal added to a tin of beans or leftover runner beans or a salad of lettuce, tomato, spring onions, cucumber, peppers; add black pepper and a squeeze of lemon or lime juice. Serve with baked potato if liked.

Stir-fried king prawns With brown rice, stir-fried vegetables and, for a treat, sweet chilli sauce.

Kedgeree Brown rice, with chopped hard-boiled egg, peas and flaked fish such as haddock.

Red snapper in tomato sauce Red snapper, simmered with lime or lemon juice, black pepper, chopped peppers and tinned tomatoes, served with rice and/or fresh vegetables.

Vegetables

Roast vegetables A selection of vegetables such as red, green and yellow peppers, a few baby potatoes, parsnips, carrots, sweet potatoes, leeks, cut into chunks and roasted in olive oil in the oven. Or skewer the vegetables on kebab sticks before roasting. Also delicious with sweet chilli sauce!

Stir-fried vegetables Stir-fry in olive oil some vegetables, such as halved baby carrots, baby sweetcorn, mangetout and bean sprouts. As a dressing, try orange zest, soy sauce or sweet chilli sauce.

Desserts

Naughty fruit salad Fresh fruit salad as liked. Marinate in rum, or add a few chocolate buttons from your treats! Kiwi fruit, melon and grapes make a lovely exotic fruit salad.

Chocolate surprise A few chocolate buttons from your treats with a bowl of strawberries or grapes.

Nutty fruit salad Fresh fruit salad with nuts and raisins.

Banana boat Slice a banana lengthways and through the middle add finely chopped fruit salad and/or raisins, sunflower seeds or finely chopped nuts as liked. For a treat drizzle with rum, brandy or a liqueur.

Fried banana Thickly slice a banana and shallow fry in a smear of light olive oil.

Fruit and cheese Cube your favourite cheeses and add some chopped fruit, such as an apple, some strawberries or grapes. Try a fruit salad with cubed cheese and nuts.

Useful addresses

Anorexia and Bulimia Care
PO Box 173
Letchworth
Hertfordshire SG6 1XQ
Tel.: 01462 423351
Helpline for parents or those supporting school-age children only: 01934 710336 (9.30 a.m. to 4.30 p.m. each weekday except Wednesdays)
Website: www.anorexiabulimiacare.co.uk
Email: mail@anorexiabulimiacare.co.uk

A national charity with a Christian foundation working to support all those who struggle because of eating disorders and related problems. Staffed mainly by those who have recovered and understand what callers are going through.

The British Dietetic Association
5th Floor, Charles House
148–149 Great Charles Street
Queensway
Birmingham B3 3HT
Tel.: 0121 200 8080
Website: www.bdaweightwise.com
Email: info@bda.uk.com

The British Nutrition Foundation
High Holborn House
52–54 High Holborn
London WC1V 6RQ
Tel.: 020 7404 6504 (multiple lines)
Website: www.nutrition.org.uk
Email: postbox@nutrition.org.uk

Caraline (Eating Disorders Counselling and Support Service)
Kline House
13 George Street West
Luton LU1 2BJ
Helpline: 01582 457474
Website: www.caraline.com
Email: caralineed@aol.com

Eating Disorders Association
First Floor, Wensum House
103 Prince of Wales Road
Norwich NR1 1DW
Tel.: 01603 619090
Helpline: 0845 634 1414 for adults: 0845 634 7650 for under-18s
Website: www.edauk.com
Email: info@edauk.com

Eating Disorders Research Unit
Institute of Psychiatry
De Crespigny Park
London SE5 8AF
Tel.: 020 7836 5454
Website: www.eatingresearch.com
Email: edu@iop.kcl.ac.uk

First Steps to Freedom
PO Box 476
Newquay
Cornwall TR7 1WQ
Helpline: 0845 120 2916
Website: www.first-steps.org
Email: first.steps@btconnect.com

Provides information and support for people experiencing all types of
anxiety disorders.

International Eating Disorders Centre
119–121 Wendover Road
Aylesbury
Bucks HP21 9LW
Tel.: 01296 330557
Website: www.eatingdisorderscentre.co.uk
Email: enquiries@eatingdisorderscentre.co.uk

National Centre for Eating Disorders
54 New Road
Esher
Surrey KT10 9NU
Helpline: 0845 838 2040
Website: www.eating-disorders.org.uk
Email: ncfed@btclick.com

National Obesity Forum
PO Box 6625
Nottingham NG2 5PA
Tel.: 0115 8462109 (Monday to Friday, 8.30 a.m. to 5 p.m.)
Website: www.nationalobesityforum.org.uk
Email: info@nationalobesityforum.org.uk

The Obesity Awareness & Solutions Trust (TOAST)
Latton Bush Centre
Southern Way
Harlow
Essex CM18 7BL
Tel.: 01279 866010 (Monday to Friday, 9 a.m. to 5 p.m.)
Helpline: 0845 045 0225
Website: www.toast-uk.org
Email: enquiries@toast-uk.org.uk

OCD Action
22–24 Highbury Grove
Suite 107
London N5 2EA
Tel.: 0870 360 OCDA (6232) (Office)
Helpline: 0845 045 0225 (Monday to Friday, 9 a.m. to 5 p.m.)
Website: www.ocdaction.org.uk
Email: info@ocdaction.org.uk

Helps those with obsessive–compulsive disorder (OCD), body dismorphic disorder (BDD) and other related conditions.

Overeaters Anonymous
PO Box 19
Stretford
Manchester M32 9EB
Tel.: 07000 784985
Website: www.oagb.org.uk
Email: oagbnsb@hotmail.com

Provides advice on all types of eating disorder.

Useful US websites

www.hazelden.org

Provides support for those in a situation of addiction, including treatment, publishing, education, research and help towards recovery. Four treatment centres in the USA.

www.usdrugrehabcenters.com

www.foodaddicts.org

www.foodaddiction.com

Further reading

Carlson, Neil R. et al., *Psychology*. Allyn and Bacon, Boston MA, 2000.

Cordain, Loren, *The Paleo Diet*. John Wiley & Sons, New York, 2003.

Elliot-Wright, Susan, *Coping with Type 2 Diabetes*. Sheldon Press, London, 2005.

Gazzola, Alex, *Living with Food Allergy*. Sheldon Press, London, 2005.

Gazzola, Alex, *Living with Food Intolerance*. Sheldon Press, London, 2004.

Harcombe, Zoe, *Why Do You Overeat? When All You Want is to be Slim*. Accent Press, Pembroke Dock, 2004.

Katherine, Anne, *Anatomy of a Food Addiction: The Brain Chemistry of Overeating*. Gürze Books, Carlsbad CA, 2003.

Lewin, Roger, *Human Evolution*. Blackwell Publishing, Oxford, 2004.

Sheppard, Kay, *Food Addiction: Healing Day by Day*. Health Communications, Deerfield Beach FL, 2003.

Sheppard, Kay, *From the First Bite: A Complete Guide to Recovery from Food Addiction*. Health Communications, Deerfield Beach FL, 2000.

Somer, Elizabeth, *The Origin Diet*. Owl Books, New York, 2002.

Vander, Arthur et al., *Human Physiology: The Mechanisms of Body Function*. McGraw-Hill Education, Boston MA, 2001.

Index